INTRODUCTION	4-12	FOOD AND DRINK	109-110
THE AEGEAN COAST	13-44	SHOPPING	110
THE MEDITERRANEAN	45-60	ACCOMMODATION	110-111
CENTRAL TURKEY	61-70	NIGHTLIFE	111
ISTANBUL	71-88	HOW TO BE A LOCAL	111
THE BLACK SEA	89-92	FESTIVALS	112
EASTERN TURKEY	93-96	CLIMATE	112
PEACE AND QUIET – Turkey's Wildlife and Countryside	97-108	DIRECTORY	113-121
		LANGUAGE: Useful words & phrases	122-124
		INDEX	125

This book employs a simple rating system to help choose which places to visit:

◆◆◆   do not miss

◆◆   see if you can

◆   worth seeing if you have time

INTRODUCTION

For many thousands of years Turkey has been one of the principal crossroads of the world: a place where camel caravans trekked from the East towards the city now known as Istanbul, delivering spices and silks for the market-places of the West.

Yet until quite recently this vast country, which spans both Europe and Asia, was virtually unknown as a holiday destination, her 5,000 miles (8,000km) of delightful coastline, picture-postcard fishing ports, crystal-clear seas and staggering scenery all but overlooked by the holiday-going public.

Instead, Turkey has been the preserve of 'travellers' as opposed to holiday-makers: people attracted by her myriad reminders of past civilisations: opulent sultans' palaces, Ottoman mosques, awe-inspiring archaeological sites, troglodyte cave-dwellings and ancient thermal pools. People who were happy to forgo

The inner wall of the old medieval fortress of Alanya still keeps watch over what is probably the most picturesque of all the old fishing towns along the Turkish Mediterranean coast

Essential
Turkey

by

GERRY CRAWSHAW

Gerry Crawshaw has been writing about Turkey's holiday
delights since first discovering them in the early 1970s, and
has since acquired an intimate knowledge of the country,
especially its increasingly popular coastal resorts.

Produced by the Publishing Division of
The Automobile Association

Written by Gerry Crawshaw
Peace and Quiet Section by Paul
Sterry
Consultant: Frank Dawes

Edited, designed and produced by
the Publishing Division of The
Automobile Association. Maps © The
Automobile Association 1990

Distributed in the United Kingdom
by the Publishing Division of The
Automobile Association, Fanum
House, Basingstoke, Hampshire,
RG21 2EA

The contents of this publication are
believed correct at the time of
printing. Nevertheless, the publishers
cannot accept responsibility for
errors or omissions, nor for changes
in details given.

© The Automobile Association 1990

All rights reserved. No part of this
publication may be reproduced,
stored in a retrieval system, or
transmitted in any form or by any
means – electronic, photocopying,
recording, or otherwise – unless the
written permission of the publishers
has been obtained beforehand.

A CIP catalogue record for this book
is available from the British Library.

ISBN 0 86145 866 4

Published by The Automobile
Association

Typesetting: Tradespools Ltd, Frome,
Somerset
Colour separation: Mullis Morgan,
London
Printing: Printers S.R.L., Trento, Italy

creature comforts and for whom soaking up the sun on a beach held little or no interest.

But suddenly, practically overnight, Turkey has burst upon the holiday scene as a major contender in the sun, sea and sand stakes. Tired of the traditional Mediterranean sunspots, and lured by incessant newspaper, magazine and television reports of Turkey's incredibly low prices, holiday-makers are flocking to the country's coastal regions in ever increasing numbers, and the upsurge looks set to accelerate in the coming years. Major travel companies have leapt on the bandwagon with package holidays aimed specifically at those who care little for Turkey's rich historical past but for whom the idea of heaven is hours of doing nothing, or at least not very much, on a sun-blessed beach.

It is a trend which the Turkish authorities are greeting with mixed feelings. For while they are delighted with the unprecedented worldwide interest in Turkey's holiday attractions and the important and much-needed foreign currency this is generating, they are anxious to avoid turning the country into a carbon-copy of other mass-market holiday destinations, or falling into the trap of allowing the kind of monstrous concrete skyscraper hotels that blight many a Mediterranean coastline.

That said, touristic development is proceeding at a phenomenal pace, especially along Turkey's Mediterranean and Aegean coasts, with new hotels, holiday villages, self-catering apartments, restaurants, bars, discothèques—even brand new, purpose-built holiday resorts—springing up like mushrooms. Airports, roads and other aspects of infrastructure are all coming in for major development and improvements, too, with the result that Turkey is increasingly able to cope with the growing bands of holiday-makers looking for a 'new' destination, with sun as the chief objective.

Historic Sites

Straddling both Europe and Asia, Turkey has been a popular battleground over the ages, playing host to many great empires from the Bronze Age Hittites, Classical Greece and Rome to the Turkish Ottomans. Myth and legend have become entwined with history and tales abound; not surprising when you consider the cast includes Helen of Troy, Jason and the Argonauts, King Midas, Alexander the Great, Antony and Cleopatra and Ottoman sultans such as Mehmet the Conqueror. The impressive remains of Turkey's remarkable history are to be found throughout the country.

A Brief History

The earliest signs of civilisation in Turkey go back to the 6th millennium BC, and it was here that some of the world's first cities were built. Hittite peoples from what was to become the USSR had settled the coast of Asia Minor (as Turkey was known until recent times) by the 13th century BC, and went on to become the undisputed rulers of the whole Near East. That empire eventually collapsed, and Asia Minor became a patchwork of tribes and states with such names as Phrygians, Scythians, Lydians, Assyrians, Persians and Greeks. In time the Persians became dominant, but the Greeks kept their European strongholds, and, at the near-

The ruins of the once-great city of Pergamon, which flourished during the 2nd century BC, attracts many visitors. Its theatre could hold about 15,000 people

legendary battles of Marathon and Salamis, defeated the Persians. Alexander the Great conquered the key cities of Miletus and Ephesus and captured all the cities of the Persian Empire. The next empire to take Asia Minor for its own was the Roman, with the first troops arriving in 201BC. For 600 years Asia Minor was a pivot of the Roman Empire, and in AD330 Constantine moved his capital from Rome to Byzantium, renamed Constantinople. The Byzantine Empire flourished, reaching a pinnacle under Justinian in the 6th century.

In about AD800 tribespeople (principally the Seljuks) who were eventually to become the Turks of today, began an inexorable westward migration from their homelands in Mongolia, Afghanistan and Turkestan. In 1071 they won a great victory against the Byzantine army in eastern Turkey, and eventually arrived at the walls of Constantinople. Before they could take the capital they themselves were overwhelmed by Moghuls, who divided the area into small provinces, one of which, around Bursa, was ruled by the Ottoman dynasty. The Ottomans rapidly gained in power, until by the beginning of the 14th century, they controlled the whole of western Asia Minor. Constantinople remained a Christian bastion in an area that by now had become almost wholly Muslim until 1402, when it went under siege. When it fell at last the Byzantine Empire was ended and, renamed Istanbul, it became the capital of the Ottoman Empire.

By the 16th century, and particularly under Suleyman the Great, the Ottoman Empire had become one of the world's great powers, but its expanding ambitions eventually brought it into conflict with the principal European states. At the same time internal conflicts weakened the Empire, and by the 19th century it was in decline and being attacked on all sides. It struggled on until 1923 when Mustafa Kemal (Ataturk – 'the father of the Turks') took control of the country.

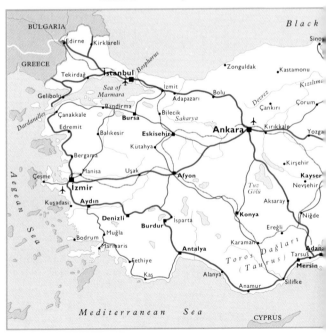

Singlehandedly, he wrenched Turkey into the 20th century. In 1952 Turkey joined NATO, but in the late 1950s the country fell into political trouble which has continued on and off until now. Under General Evran, Turkey is once again poised for a democratic future, and an economic future tied with the European community.

Special Interest Holidays
Given the variety of Turkey's assets there are numerous special interest options open to the holiday-maker looking for more than just a chance to laze on a beach enjoying the sun with only an occasional foray to an ancient site. Watersports are the most popular of these, including windsurfing, waterskiing, diving and dinghy sailing. Resorts that are particularly well equipped for these activities include Marmaris, Bodrum, Bitez, Kusadasi, Kemer and Foca. Sailing holidays along Turkey's Aegean and Mediterranean coasts are also in enormous

demand now, especially aboard the traditional Turkish wooden boats known as *gulets* or ketches. These are made by craftsmen in boatyards located along the two coasts, and are specially designed for coastal cruising. Particularly popular are the itineraries known as 'Blue Cruises'.

Walking and trekking can be a real delight in Turkey, especially near Kemer and Alanya, while birdwatchers are also being increasingly catered for by the holiday companies.

A growing number of visitors are also discovering Turkey's thermal spas, long enjoyed by Turks themselves for their therapeutic and healing powers. Top resorts include Bursa, Cesme, Pamukkale and Yalova.

What to expect

The very fact that Turkey is new to the mass holiday business means that standards are often not what visitors may have come to expect. The overall standards of public utilities, hygiene, drainage and services, for instance, are usually rather less sophisticated than those found in many other holiday countries. As an example, visitors should be prepared for Turkish-style bathrooms where the shower water drains away through a simple hole set in the middle of the floor—but only after flooding the bathroom first! Hot water cannot always be guaranteed, and water shortages in the peak summer months frequently occur.

Most Turkish hotels are clean and reasonably well equipped, but while the majority offer bedrooms with European-style furnishing, visitors opting for lower grade hotels and *pensions* should not be surprised if they are confronted with a row of pegs on the wall, instead of a wardrobe, since traditionally the Turks do not use wardrobes. Another point to bear in mind is that bedrooms, especially in the older-style hotels and self-catering apartments, are usually very small.

Outside the main resorts, there are numerous unmade, unlit roads, often little more than dirt tracks, leading to new holiday developments, so it is wise to take a torch with you for use in the evenings. Since tourism in Turkey is just taking off, many of the resorts are expanding to cope

Away from the modern, cosmopolitan cities and resorts, life in Turkey continues much as it has always done

with the ever-increasing demand for accommodation. As a result, building work is an ongoing activity, and the peace and quiet of a holiday can by no means be assumed.

Another disconcerting trend is for the provision of unnecessarily loud music at practically every open-air bar, restaurant or *lokanta*, no matter how peaceful and idyllic the setting.

No holiday destination, however, is without its drawbacks, and the inconveniences the visitor to Turkey is likely to experience pale into insignificance compared with the delights that lie in store: the superb weather, beaches, food, memorable excursions, the friendliness of a people for whom hospitality is a way of life, and the amazing value for money.

In this book, where appropriate, hotels and restaurants which enjoy good reputations are mentioned; the listings are selective rather than comprehensive, for the simple reason that Turkey's holiday industry is developing at a tremendous pace, with new establishments entering the field practically every day, especially in the up-and-coming coastal resorts. Those listed are now well established, and usually offer reliable standards.

Likewise, the information given for motorists is not as comprehensive as that in guidebooks for many other popular holiday destinations, again for the simple reason that travel to Turkey by car is a mammoth undertaking for all but the most intrepid. Car hire within Turkey is, however, growing in popularity, despite its high cost, so there is information and helpful tips for those who fancy picking up a car on arrival or hiring one for a few days.

The majority of holiday-makers awakening to Turkey's attractions head for the resorts on her Aegean and Mediterranean shores, where the facilities and amenities are of a sufficiently high standard overall to ensure an enjoyable holiday. For this reason, greater prominence is given to resorts in these areas rather than those on Turkey's Black Sea coast which, though attractive and having much to offer the visitor, is comparatively underdeveloped when it comes to international tourism and, on the whole, lacks the type of facilities today's holiday-makers have come to expect.

Turkey is the last great unspoilt coastline in the Mediterranean, where you can relax on comparatively uncrowded beaches, swim in secluded coves, feast on world-renowned cuisine, enjoy spectacular scenery, search for bargains in colourful shops and bazaars, or simply soak up the atmosphere of a western land with one face turned east.

Istanbul's enormous covered market, the Grand Bazaar, a vast labyrinth of narrow passages containing between 4,000 and 6,000 little shops, was first created in the 15th century

THE AEGEAN COAST

Turkey's lovely Aegean region offers something for everyone—sunlover, nature-lover, photographer, sightseer. Its shores abound in sandy beaches, sheltered coves and rocky bays lapped by blue, clean, crystal waters, and it is here that you will find some of the most popular, longest established and most picturesque resorts in the whole country—such as Bodrum, Marmaris and Kusadasi—as well as brand new but fast-developing beach resorts such as Altinkum, with its beautiful golden sands.

The coast is also richly adorned with pretty fishing villages and the remains of many once-great cities. Here lie the ruins of the great city of Pergamon (now known as Bergama), which possessed one of the largest libraries in the ancient world, containing 200,000 volumes. Not far from Pergamon's acropolis are the ruins of one of the most important medical centres of the Classical world.

Further south is the capital of the Turkish Aegean, Izmir, the birthplace of Homer. This modern city with its palm-lined avenues and excellent hotels, boasts one of the finest natural harbours in Turkey. To the north of Izmir is the resort of Ayvalik, with lovely beaches and pine forests, and the little resort of Foca, whose inhabitants found and colonised such towns as Marseilles and Nice. West of Izmir lies the bigger and more developed resort of Cesme, with its thermal springs and yacht marina, while to the south of

The 4th century BC architects of the Temple of Apollo at Didim intended it to be the Eighth Wonder of the World

Izmir is Kusadasi, one of the region's premier resorts, conveniently located for sightseeing and excursions to the many classical sites in the area.

In the centre of Turkey's west coast is the region of ancient Ionia, boasting such ruins as Ephesus, Miletus and Didim, all reflecting the timeless grace of Ionian architecture. Chief among these Ionian cities is Ephesus, one-time Roman capital of Asia, and of which St Paul once asked 'Is there a greater city?' Along Ephesus' Arcadian Way, Mark Antony and Cleopatra once rode in procession; in the city's great theatre St Paul preached against the goddess Artemis; and in a little house outside the city the Virgin Mary is believed to have spent her last days. Also in Ephesus stood one of the Seven

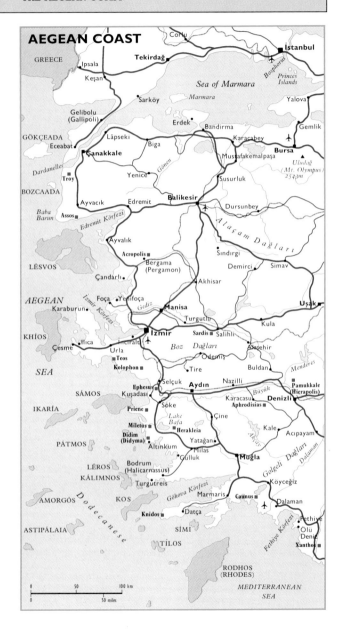

Wonders of the Ancient World, the Temple of Artemis.

In addition to these splendid man-made wonders, the Turkish Aegean offers a rich assortment of natural wonders, not least the calcified waterfall of Pamukkale, known as 'Cotton Castle', where thermal spring water laden with calcium carbonate running off the plateau's edge has formed a sparkling white petrified cascade of basins ringed by stalactites. Behind the waterfall lie the ruins of the once great Roman city of Hierapolis.

On the southwest of the Aegean coast are the popular resorts of Bodrum, Marmaris, Datca, Fethiye and Dalyan.

The hot summer temperatures that are a feature of Turkey's Aegean coast are, happily, tempered by gentle, refreshing sea breezes, while the rugged landscape is surprisingly green and luxuriant thanks to the many fig orchards and olive groves found here.

ALTINKUM

Less than five years ago Altinkum was just a small hamlet located behind a wide sandy bay. Today, it is developing into one of Turkey's most popular, purpose-built beach resorts, with a good choice of brand new accommodation and no shortage of *lokantas*, cafés, bars and lively night-time diversions for when sunlovers have had enough of the resort's principal attraction, its magnificent beach.

At one end of the bay is a rocky headland, and beyond it is a series of coves backed by unspoilt, verdant countryside.

There is another cove at the other end, this one sheltered and with fine sand, while about half a mile beyond is yet another series of fine sandy bays, all small, peaceful and unpolluted. Watersports lovers are particularly well catered for in Altinkum, with professional instruction in windsurfing and other activities readily and inexpensively available. Conditions are excellent for both beginners and the more experienced, the water being shallow and usually warm.

Lokantas, ice cream parlours, bars and shops are to be found fronting the main bay for most of its length, all offering good value for money. Competition among the many small restaurants springing up to serve the needs of the growing bands of holiday-makers making a bee-line for Altinkum is fierce, so it is difficult to spend more than a trifling amount on a meal, and a sumptuous one at that!

Hotels and Restaurants

Of the smaller, simpler hotels, the **Three Mevsim**, located about ten minutes' walk from the beach, has a colourful small terrace on which breakfasts are served and where barbecues are a regular feature. Many of the new hotels under construction promise excellent facilities and standards.

Excursion from Altinkum

DIDIM

The village now known as Didim, which lies only a few miles from Altinkum, was once called Didyma, and it was here that the ancient Greeks built a magnificent temple dedicated to the god Apollo, twin brother of Artemis. The original temple was destroyed by the Persians in 494BC and remained in ruins until Seleucus I of Syria began its restoration 200 years later, a feat that took no fewer than 600 years to accomplish, and even then not entirely.

Didyma itself was never a city but the site of a famous oracle, who was consulted by everyone from beggars to emperors. Unseen by anyone but the temple priests, the oracle would fast for three days and breathe the vapours emanating from the sacred spring. This seemingly put her in a state of divine inspiration, whereupon she passed obscure messages to the priests who, in turn, translated them for their clients. Oracles flourished at Didyma until the Byzantines adopted Christianity as the state religion.

Of the numerous remains to be seen in Didim, the most impressive are of the Temple of Apollo, whose entrance is marked by a lion. A monumental stairway leads up to a forest of 103 remarkably well-preserved Ionian columns.
End of excursion

◆◆◆
AYVALIK

Ayvalik is charmingly situated, with some 23 islands nestling in its bay and a coastline edged with pine forests and heavily indented with attractive coves. Largely unspoilt by tourism, this small Turkish seaside town does not, as yet, cater for visitors looking for a lively nightlife. For the present, a walk through its twisting, high-walled streets is like stepping back in time, with tantalising glimpses through open doors to marble workshops and carpenters at work. Architecture in this town is an intricate blend of colours and designs, the skyline broken by both chimneys and minarets— twin symbols of the dual nature of a traditional fishing town that also relies on light industry for its survival.

With its thriving olive and soap-making industries, Ayvalik has long been a popular holiday spot with Turkish visitors, and is now attracting increasing numbers of visitors from other countries.

Beaches
There are places to swim in and around the town, but some five miles or so south from the centre is Sarimsakli—an attractive stretch of beach lined with holiday accommodation as well as café-bars.

Hotels and Restaurants
There are several smallish hotels in and around the town, the **Baskent Motel**, at Sarimsakli, being particularly good value. Ayvalik also offers a good choice of restaurants, but most visitors venture at least once to sample the seafood specialities of the restaurants of Alibey, an island just across the bay from Ayvalik, linked to the mainland by a causeway. The charming waterfront here has a small harbour sporting gaily painted boats and fringed with restaurants, some offering live entertainment.
Tourism Bureau: Yat Limani Karsisi (tel: (311) 2122).

BODRUM

Bodrum is one of Turkey's best known and longest established holiday resorts, noted for its excellent facilities and amenities, cosmopolitan atmosphere and lively nightlife. A picture-postcard resort often referred to as the St Tropez of the eastern Aegean, it is particularly popular with younger holiday-makers, though with its wide range of shops, restaurants, bars and discos, colourful and lively port and yacht marina, it is a favourite resort with all age groups.

The ancient name of Bodrum was Halicarnassus, and it was founded in the 5th century BC as one of the great colonies of Greece. Its most famous citizen was Herodotus, known as the Father of History, who was born here in 485BC.

The golden age of Halicarnassus occurred in the 4th century BC, when the ruling king of the region, Mausolus of Caria, made the town his capital. When he died his wife-sister Artemisia succeeded him and built a memorial to her husband so vast and elaborate that it was subsequently declared one of the Seven Wonders of the Ancient World. Little remains of the structure itself, but the original site of the mausoleum can be found on the outskirts of the town.

The town has a distinctly laid-back atmosphere, and one has the feeling that here, unlike anywhere else in Turkey, practically 'anything goes'. Despite the absence of notable beaches in the resort itself, its

Bodrum has been deservedly popular with holiday-makers for years

beautiful setting has led to its development into a lively place with a wealth of modern tourist facilities. Yet notwithstanding the continuing development, with new hotels and holiday apartments springing up practically overnight, it still manages to retain a distinct village charm. Tiers of dazzling cube-shaped, whitewashed houses ablaze with a profusion of flowers rise up from the harbour, where floating gin palaces jostle with quaint fishing boats and the stylish *gulet* wooden boats, which are built here in the resort.

Castle

The focal point is the magnificent 15th-century castle of St Peter, perched on a promontory dividing the two bays around which the town is set. Now housing a museum and open-air theatre, it is a treasure trove of the fruits of salvage operations off the local coast, some of which date back 1,000 years. Construction of the castle began some time after 1402 when Tamerlane took the city and the Knights of St John consequently lost their fortress there. It was actually built on an island, but since then the island has become linked to the mainland. The castle's five towers and the gothic chapel have all been carefully restored. The English Tower has been furnished with reproductions of tapestries, furniture, weapons and armour of the 15th century, giving the visitor an excellent idea of the life of those times. The courtyards of the castle are adorned with plants and trees

The crusaders' impressive castle dominates the beautifully-sited port of Bodrum, formerly Halicarnassus, founded by Dorian Greeks

which relate to ancient times, while peacocks strut amid oleanders and statues. The French and Italian Towers and the gothic chapel are used as archaeological museums, displaying objects taken from sites around Bodrum. The best known of the museums, that of Underwater Archaeology,

contains valuable objects recovered since 1968 from expeditions in the Aegean and Mediterranean Seas. There are pieces of the hull and parts of the cargo of a Byzantine ship that sank about AD620; the wreck of a Bronze Age ship which went down about 1200 or 1300BC; and the wreck of an Islamic ship which was loaded with glass.

Mausoleum

Just round the corner from the castle are the remains of the first ever mausoleum, built in 376BC. Much of this Wonder of the Ancient World was dismantled by one of Bodrum's earliest visitors, Sir Charles Newton, and shipped to the British Museum in London.

Bazaar

On the other side of the castle is Bodrum's own bazaar, a narrow street featuring scores of restaurants and bars, tiny shops selling fine leather, jewellery and beachware. At any time of the day or night there is always something going on here.

Beaches

The town beach is, to put it mildly, uninspiring. As compensation, from the colourful and elegant yacht harbour you can catch a boat to one of the many lovely coves near by—some of them practically deserted—or you can take a *dolmus* taxi to the sandy beaches of numerous little developing resorts such as Gumbet or Ortakent, only a short distance away round the bay.

Boat Trips

One of the best boat trips is a day exploring nearby Orak island, where fantastically clear water offers marvellous possibilities for swimmers, especially with snorkelling equipment. The boats continue on to Karaada, where you can bathe in beautifully warm sulphur springs.

Also not to be missed is the breathtakingly lovely Gulf of Gokova and the scenic serpentine route along the Datca peninsula, while in high season you can visit the Greek island of Kos for the day.

THE AEGEAN COAST

Hotels

The **TMT Hotel** and the **Milta Torba** holiday village are both well run and have excellent reputations. At the nearby beach resort of Gumbet, the **Metemtur** holiday village promises to be one of the most attractive and stylish in the area, and enjoys a quiet location on a lovely, unspoilt bay. Also to be recommended is the **Hotel Manastir**, constructed from the ruins of an old monastery, and located high on a hill overlooking the marina.

Discothèques

Bodrum is renowned for its nightlife. Of its many discothèques, the one which stands out most is the **Halikarnas**, built in the form of an amphitheatre by the sea. As night progresses the Halikarnas lights up quite literally, with lasers projecting a spectacular display over the bay. One of the most sophisticated night spots in the whole of Turkey, it is a big hit with the young and trendy. Once a week there is a folklore show here, with Turkish cuisine, folk performances and belly dancing.

Tourism Bureau: 12 Eylul Meyd (tel: (6141) 1091). On the main harbour square, near the castle wall.

Bodrum Peninsula

Bodrum's ever-growing popularity as a holiday resort has been seized upon by many of the

Bodrum has developed into a lively modern resort catering for the tourist's every need, including all manner of souvenirs

small beach settlements dotting the large peninsula on which it is located. As a result, many holiday-makers are choosing to stay in these fast developing small resorts, taking *dolmus* taxis into Bodrum for sightseeing or night-time diversions; while there is a constant flow of traffic in the opposite direction, with Bodrum-based holiday-makers spending the day on the beaches of the little resorts, and returning to Bodrum in the late afternoon. Distances obviously vary, but it usually takes about 10 minutes from Gumbet to Bodrum, or half an hour from the more outlying resorts.

Gumbet

Gumbet is the closest beach resort, and has plenty to offer families, couples and groups. It has a relaxed, easy-going ambience, with a long stretch of coarse, golden sand shelving gently into a warm sea, making it a great favourite with children and younger holiday-makers. The pensions, hotels and bars which line the beach offer sunshades and loungers, and many of them have colourful gardens where you can relax with a beer or a glass of tea. The afternoon breeze provides good windsurfing conditions and there is no shortage of opportunities to learn or improve your skills at this or at waterskiing, sailing or even scuba diving. Dinghies, canoes and pedaloes are also available for hire, and are not expensive.

Turgutreis

Turgutreis is another fast expanding beach resort whose growing popularity owes not a little to the fact that it is only 12 miles (19km) from Bodrum. It is also popular with holiday-makers who appreciate the opportunity of getting a little closer to the Turkish people, for here you encounter farmers, fishermen and weavers all going about their daily work, and wizened old men sitting at shaded tables drinking tea, playing cards and gossiping. On the long, clean beach there are loungers and sombrero-styled sunshades to rent, while for a change of pace there are the distractions of a town square, a playground and a market.

The approach to Turgutreis from Bodrum is particularly pleasant, since it enjoys a delightful green setting encircling a bay marked with islands. Named after Turgut Reis, who was born here and later became a Turkish admiral during the 16th century, the resort is, after Bodrum, the next largest settlement on the peninsula.

On the small waterfront promenade down by the square there are seats where you can sit over a drink while you admire the view across the bay. From the harbour, which is dotted with fishing boats, you can join a boat trip to the other areas of the peninsula or to Rabbit Island.

Ortakent

Ortakent is a charming, small seaside resort on the Bodrum peninsula, in a countryside setting of fig, orange and mandarin orchards. Wandering through the village you will see some fine examples of older-style Turkish architecture—such

THE AEGEAN COAST

Although it has a lot to offer in the way of sailing and other watersports, Bitez remains quiet and unspoilt

as the Mustafa Pasa Tower which was built in 1601—while crowning the hill like sentinels as they gaze out to sea are old windmills.

A partly shaded road runs through the village for a little less than a mile before ending at the beach, a fairly long stretch of sand and pebbles bathed by calm waters. Here you can windsurf, hire a canoe or join an organised boat trip to a secluded bay or cove. Along the beach there are a couple of boat-building yards with builders at work—a craft which has been passed on down through generations.

Shopping requirements are catered for in a few mini-markets in the village, while for a change of pace, scenery and atmosphere the sophisticated attractions of Bodrum Town are within easy reach by *dolmus* taxi.

Bitez
Bitez is a rural, quiet and unsophisticated beach resort where small hotels, *pensions* and bars line the shingle and sand shore, and there are numerous small jetties for swimming and sunbathing. If you want to try your hand at windsurfing, this is one of the places for you—brightly coloured sails stretch out on the sand and water as far as the eye can see. Behind the beach, a short walk away, a tangle of small lanes winding through tangerine groves offer a picturesque alternative to lazing on the beach.

Akyarlar
A tiny fishing hamlet about half an hour's drive from Bodrum, Akyarlar comprises a few houses, *pensions*, grocery shops and bars, and is a 'get-away-from-it' retreat recommended to those who relish comparative tranquillity and a friendly atmosphere.

Along the road which runs on from Turgutreis to Akyarlar is a series of small bays and uncrowded beaches. The narrow strip of beach near the tiny harbour just below the village of Akyarlar shelves gently, while just around the bay is 'Black Fig' beach and a beach-side restaurant: a popular spot for pleasure crafts and daytrippers.

There are organised boat trips from the village to neighbouring resorts, and Bodrum Town can be reached via Turgutreis.

Golkoy

A small farming community and beach resort, Golkoy stretches along the shore of a little-known bay about 20 minutes north of Bodrum by *dolmus* taxi and is a good base from which to visit other delightful bays around the peninsula. One of the chief attractions of Golkoy is its village atmosphere, with the possibility of quiet walks among old farm buildings and the opportunity of living among a mainly Turkish community away from crowds and mass tourism.

Guvercinlik

Guvercinlik, which means 'the place where doves come to roost', is another small unsophisticated resort nestling in a sheltered bay about 15 miles (24km) from Bodrum. Facilities in the resort include a general store, post office and a fruit and vegetable stall. There are no real beaches here, but swimming from the jetty is popular. Just a few miles west of the resort are numerous little coves indenting this beautiful stretch of coastline, which are ideal for escapists and families in search of peace and quiet.

CESME

Cesme is one of Turkey's premier holiday resorts and one of its longest established. In the centre, little tumbledown houses are tucked away in quaint streets and alleyways which run behind the harbour, and here shoemakers, carpenters and tailors follow their trade much as they did in days gone by, while there are dozens of tiny shops in which to browse.

A resort with plenty of character, Cesme is dominated by a 14th-century fortress from which there are excellent views over the harbour.

In the resort's main square the jet black statues of Hasan Pasa and the lion that symbolises his temperament stare out to sea and to the Greek island of Chios, their backs to the impressive old fortress. The smooth round walls of this Genoese stronghold butt out into the pavement of the seafront road, where a multitude of waterfront restaurants vie for trade.

During the day a small sandy cove near the harbour is a suntrap for those who don't feel inclined to catch a *dolmus* taxi to the golden sands of Altinkum, only 4 miles (6.4km) away; or to one of the best beaches in the area, on the Ilica road, just over a mile away. This wide, isolated strip of soft sand stretches for miles and is seldom crowded. Its namesake, Ilica, is a pretty marina town famed for its hot thermal baths; in fact, the name Cesme literally means 'fountain' or 'spring'.

Another place to visit is Dalyan Koy, a small fishing village much

THE AEGEAN COAST

frequented by lovers of good seafood. The setting is romantic, and you can eat in restaurants right by the water's edge. Food lovers will also appreciate Cesme's speciality: *lokma*, piping hot doughnuts popular with the locals and eaten at both breakfast and tea.

In ancient times Cesme, or Kysus as it was then known, was one of the most important cities of Ionia and it has been a major medical treatment centre and an active travel and naval base for centuries. Today, Cesme and its surroundings makes a living from tobacco, olives, citrus fruits and grape cultivation, fishing and, increasingly, from tourism. Indeed, one of the biggest holiday developments in the whole of Turkey is located here: the vast Golden Dolphin Holiday Village.

Fortress of Cesme

The fortress was enlarged, and new towers added, during its restoration in 1508 by the Ottoman Sultan Beyazit II, son of Mehmet the Conqueror. The castle and the port provided protection for the trading ships and the navy against inclement weather and enemy attacks. The south gate of the fortress is a characteristic example of Ottoman architecture.

Museum of Ottoman Arms

Located inside the fortress, this museum contains an excellent exhibition of cannons, swords, armour, pistols and rifles, most gathered from collections at Topkapi Palace, Istanbul. A gold and silver encrusted rifle, once belonging to Sultan Abdulaziz, is a prize exhibit.

Caravanserai

Built in 1529 by architect Omar, this two-storey inn which adjoins the fortress was converted into a hotel in 1986. It boasts a delightful courtyard restaurant where Turkish folklore performances are a regular feature.

Mausoleum

This 18th-century, hexagonally designed museum reflects the main characteristics of Ottoman mausoleum architecture.

Hotels and Restaurants

The enormous, 508-room **Golden Dolphin** holiday village is popular with visitors looking for plenty of amenities and facilities. However, the **Turban Hotel**, located on a superb stretch of beach is highly recommended. There is a good selection of restaurants and bars, while nightlife is varied and quite chic, with music bars as well as discothèques keeping things pulsating way into the night. **Tourism bureau:** Iskele Meyd. 8 (tel: (5492) 6653). Located at the port landing stage.

Excursions from Cesme

◆
ERYTHRAI

Fourteen miles (22km) northeast of Cesme, at Ildir, are the ruins of Erythrai, another of the important Ionian cities. Founded on the coastline of a beautiful bay dotted with small islands, Erythrai was inhabited by Cretans and Pamphylians after the Trojan War, and although the people managed to hang onto their traditions, the city eventually became part of the Ionian parliament before being overthrown by Basili de Genos.

Attractive holiday apartments and villas crowd up the hillside overlooking the harbour in Cesme

Later, the Persians attacked the city and brought about its collapse.

SIGACIK

A detour from the Izmir–Cesme road to Seferihisar leads to the village of Sigacik, a picturesque little port surrounded by fortified walls dating from the Genoese period. To the west of the Bay of Sigacik is an attractive beach from which the site of ancient Teos is easily accessible.
End of excursions

◆◆◆
DALYAN DELTA

The Dalyan Delta has leapt into prominence in recent times because its sandbar is one of the last breeding grounds in Europe of the loggerhead turtle. In view of the area's outstanding beauty, it had been earmarked for considerable touristic development, including the construction of several large hotels right where the rare turtles come ashore to lay their eggs, but thanks to pressure from conservationists, the developments have been 'revised' by the Turkish government.

The delta is reached by boat from the nearby village of Dalyan, and the most popular way of experiencing it to the full is to take one of the many organised day excursions that include a tour of the ancient city of Caunus and a swim in Lake Koycegiz.

THE AEGEAN COAST

Ancient Lycian cave-tombs, carved out of the rock, abound in Anatolia; these are at Dalyan

Hotels and Restaurants
The **Kaunos Hotel and Restaurant** in nearby Koycegiz is one of the best in the area. **Tourism bureau:** Kordon Golpark 1, Koycegiz (tel: 1703). By the waterfront.

Excursion from Dalyan

CAUNUS
Although not as spectacular as the ruins at many historic sites in Turkey, those at Caunus, reached by boat along the Dalyan Delta, are still impressive. They include a 20,000-seat theatre, affording tremendous views from the top, Roman baths with ancient piping, and the circular foundations of a small temple or pool.
End of excursion

DATCA
A picturesque fishing village at the westernmost tip of the Anatolian peninsula where the Aegean merges with the Mediterranean, Datca is rapidly becoming a popular resort due to the many yachts calling there, especially those on flotilla cruises, and to the fact that there are splendid sandy beaches

nearby. The town has considerable charm and quite a cosmopolitan atmosphere, with a variety of hotels, restaurants and shops including a couple of antique shops specialising in old carpets and wall-coverings. Off shore is a popular cruising ground for dolphins, while adjoining the beach is a lagoon fed by a freshwater stream.

Hotels

The **Dorya Hotel** is superbly located, surrounded by lovely gardens. Also recommended is the **Club Datca Tatil Koyu**, which has a pool, disco, sauna, tennis courts and watersports.
Tourism bureau: Iskele Mah, Belediye Binasi (tel: (6145) 1163).

Excursions from Datca

KNIDOS

Another of Datca's chief attractions is its proximity to the ancient ruins of Knidos, about 24 miles (38km) away. These have been allowed to decay but indicate the one-time importance of this huge city which was founded in 400BC and served as a natural refuge for sailors at the crucial point where the Aegean flows into the Mediterranean.

Knidos was a famous centre of art, birthplace of the architect Sostratos who built one of the Seven Wonders of Antiquity, the lighthouse of Alexandria, and of the mathematician Eudoxus, who was the first to measure the earth's circumference.

Under Persian rule the city thrived as a trading centre, to such an extent that the harbour was unable to handle the increase in shipping. The city was then re-sited at the tip of the peninsula, a position which offered the benefit of two natural harbours. Excavations of the ruins were first begun in 1857 by Sir Charles Newton, who had everything of major interest unearthed and sent to the British Museum in London, including a statue of the goddess Demeter. Over the years the ruins have been repeatedly plundered, leaving only the foundations of temples, two theatres, an odeon and what is known as the lion tomb.

You can take a taxi from Datca to the nearest village, then walk the 3 miles (5km) to reach the site at the extreme tip of the peninsula.

28

THE AEGEAN COAST

The driver will wait for your return journey. A better alternative is a day-long boat trip from Datca that includes stops for swimming *en route*.
Boat excursions also operate to Datca from Bodrum, and there are coach or mini-bus trips from Marmaris.
End of excursion

◆◆◆
FETHIYE
The lovely Gulf of Fethiye, its broad bay dotted with small islands and furrowed by inlets and coves, is one of the most impressive stretches of coastline in Turkey, its attractions greatly enhanced by lush, wooded mountain slopes which sweep down to the shore.
The town of Fethiye, which overlooks an attractive bay, is an ancient place crowned by the ruins of a fortress built by the Knights of the Crusades, and in the steep cliff surrounding it ancient Lycian tombs are carved out of the rock face. It is built on the site of ancient Telmessos, renowned for its wise scholars. Philip of Macedonia called on a sage from Telmessos to interpret a dream. This sage, Aristander, prophesied the birth and achievements of Alexander, and when the latter grew up the sage accompanied him on his campaigns.
Alexander took the city of Telmessos by trickery instead of force, asking the citizens to permit his musicians to enter. They agreed, and by night the musicians took over the city with spears and shields they had smuggled in. However, Alexander restored the city to its king out of respect for Aristander, leaving only one of his generals as the governor of Lycia.
Like the other Lycian cities, Telmessos was successively ruled by Egyptians, Syrians, Rhodians, Romans and Byzantines.
No excavations have been undertaken in the town itself, and few remains can be seen, since a severe earthquake completely destroyed both the ancient buildings and the Ottoman town in 1958. However, two Lycian tombs can be seen in the town, one beneath the rock tombs and another near the wharf.
Although architecturally uninspiring, Fethiye none the less has much to please the visitor. A wide promenade lined with cafés runs around its colourful harbour and small yachting marina, tables and chairs spilling out from underneath awnings and trees onto a waterfront terrace.
Most of the daytime action centres around Fethiye's open market, a riot of colours, sounds and smells, where you can buy a wide range of goods and souvenirs: colourful Turkish slippers, handmade jewellery, leather goods, and much more. Part fishing village and part market town, and situated close to beautiful countryside, Fethiye is a town full of local hustle and bustle; not exactly pretty, but certainly the sort of place that grows on you, with shops and restaurants primarily geared to locals rather than holiday-makers. The nearby coast is peppered with sandy bays.

Hotels and Restaurants

The **Likya Hotel** is well located and enjoys a reputation as one of the best hotels in town. There is no shortage of places to eat, many of the restaurants and bars in the back streets and alleys springing to life at night, together with those on the seafront, and most offer a tempting range of dishes from delicious kebabs to succulent fresh fish.

Tourism bureau: Iskele Meyd 1 (tel: (6151) 1527). By the marina.

Excursions from Fethiye

Excursions from this area are many and varied. In and around Fethiye itself are the intriguing Lycian rock tombs carved into the cliff face, or you can venture off to see the ancient sites of Patara and Xanthos.

The fascinating rock tombs near Fethiye are hewn out of a vertical cliff and have impressive decorated façades

THE AEGEAN COAST

◆◆
PATARA

An excursion to Patara — about 50 miles (80km) from Fethiye — is worthwhile on two counts, for not only is it a site of great antiquity, but it also boasts one of the best, totally unspoilt beaches in Turkey.

Once a thriving port, Patara's greatest days were during the Roman period, when it was the principal harbour in Lycia. Most of the surviving ruins date from that period, and include a theatre. Patara has been declared a protected area by the Turkish government, which

The many remains at Xanthos give a good indication of that magnificent city's long and turbulent history

means that hotel development is severely restricted, and not allowed by the beach or near the ruins, the extent of which becomes clear as you scramble among the dunes of fine, pale sand.

◆◆
XANTHOS

The Persian army entered the plain of Xanthos under the command of Harpagos, and did battle with the Xanthians. The greatly outnumbered Xanthians fought with legendary bravery against the superior Persian forces but were finally beaten and forced to retreat within the walls of their city, gathering their womenfolk, children, slaves and treasures into the fortress. This was then set on fire from below and around the walls, until destroyed by conflagration. Then the warriors of Xanthos made their final attack on the Persians, their voices raised in oaths of war, until every last man from Xanthos was killed.

Thus records Herodotus of Halicarnassus (Bodrum), and the fact that Sarpendon of Xanthos commanded Lycian troops in the Trojan War allows us to infer that Xanthos existed even earlier, in 1200BC.

This magnificent city, which lies about 40 miles (65km) from Fethiye, was rebuilt following its destruction at the hands of the Persians, but burned down once more between 475BC and 450BC, as indicated by a thick layer of ash discovered during excavations. After being ruled successively by Alexander the Great, the Ptolomeans and the Syrian monarch Antiochus III, Xanthos became the capital of the Lycian confederacy in the 2nd century *BC.*

The Romans demolished the Lycian acropolis and slaughtered the city's inhabitants, although the fact that a year later Marcus Antoninus had the city rebuilt and a monumental portal erected in the name of Emperor Vespasian indicates that relations with the Romans were later amicable. The city was abandoned during the Byzantine period after the first Arab incursion.

Xanthos was rediscovered in 1838 by an English archaeologist who had all the reliefs and archaeological finds of interest taken to London on a warship which sailed from Patara. Many works of art from the site are now on display in the Lycian room of the British Museum. The city dominated a green plain watered by the River Esen (Xanthos) and here can be seen many monuments from the Lycian, Roman and Byzantine periods.

Near the Roman theatre stand three splendid mausoleums: a Roman colonnaded tomb dating from the 1st century AD; a Lycian colonnaded tomb on a high base dating from the 4th century BC, on which was found the relief of a wrestler which predated the tomb itself; and the famous Tomb of the Harpies, whose original reliefs are now in the British Museum in London. Plastercasts taken from the originals have been replaced on the tomb.

Near the theatre are the remains of a Byzantine church and a Lycian palace, and a little further on is the Lycian pool, hollowed out of the rock. The royal terrace situated at the extremity of the acropolis overlooks the entire plain.

Calis

Because Fethiye itself doesn't have a beach, that at Calis, no more than 4 miles (6.4km) away round the bay, has readily stepped into the gap, and the little resort has become a particular favourite with watersports lovers. It offers a long, wide beach of coarse sand/shingle, cooled in the afternoons by a strong sea breeze which keeps the temperature pleasant even in the height of summer, and which makes for perfect windsurfing.

The beach is big enough to be seldom crowded, and is bordered by a road lined with cafés, restaurants, *pensions* and hotels, as well as a discothèque. Across the bay are lovely views of tiny, idyllic islands which face the coast, while majestic, lush green mountains behind give Calis a special appeal.

The little resort offers a sufficiently wide choice of restaurants and *lokantas* to satisfy most holiday-makers' requirements, while the attractions of lively Fethiye are only an inexpensive *dolmus* taxi hop away.

End of excursions

FOCA

A former pirate stronghold with an easygoing atmosphere, Foca is a quiet and attractive fishing town. A small shingle beach at one end of the bay is a popular sunspot, but the best swimming in the area can be found on the white sandy beach only 2 miles (3km) along the coast.

Foca was the ancient port of Phocaea and the northernmost Ionian settlement, noted for its harbour and seafaring men.

Tourism bureau: Ataturk Mah Foca Girisi (tel: (5431) 1222).

Excursion from Foca

PERGAMON

Within easy reach of the resort is the ancient site of Pergamon, now known as Bergama—one of the most impressive Classical sites in Turkey. It lies just outside the town of Bergama, where there is an excellent museum set in a delightful garden. Of particular interest to visitors is the library which once held 200,000 books, competing with that in Alexandria. It is said that Mark Antony creamed the best of the collection and gave it to Cleopatra as a present.

During the city's greatest period a gymnasium was built and also an altar to Zeus. More than a thousand figures, half animal and half human, were represented in a series of reliefs, celebrating the triumph of good over evil. The theatre here has 80 tiers of seats capable of holding 10,000. Also impressive is the Asclepion, the ancient health centre which experimented in the healing powers of herbs and sacred waters. It was considered to be one of the finest centres of its kind in the world providing cures for bodily and spiritual ills.
End of excursion

A romantic sunset across Izmir Bay

IZMIR

Izmir is a pleasant city with palm-lined boulevards, a lively atmosphere, excellent hotels and shops, and plenty to interest the visitor, including first-rate seaside restaurants, museums, a cultural park, and a bazaar offering a wide variety of antiques, jewellery and clothing. Turkey's third largest port and her third largest city, with a population of approximately 2,350,000, it is impressively situated at the end of a large gulf ringed by mountains and, though

Moorish style. From here you can walk through the little streets to the bazaar, which is usually very lively and colourful. Close to the bazaar are three attractive mosques, the Kemeralti Camii, Hisar Camii and Sadirvan Camii, plus two 17th-century caravanserais.

Roman Agora
Not far from the bazaar are the imposing remains of the Roman agora (market place), dating from the 2nd century AD. Several portals lead on to the square, where you can see statues of Poseidon, Demeter and Artemis.

Velvet Castle
Kadifekale, the Velvet Castle, dominates Izmir from the top of Mount Pagos. It was on this mountain that, according to legend, Nemeses appeared to Alexander the Great in a dream and told him to found a city on this site and encourage the inhabitants of the old city of Izmir to move here. The original fortress was constructed by Lysimachus, one of Alexander the Great's generals, and it was later restored by the Romans and the Byzantines. From the castle there is a magnificent panorama of the city and bay of Izmir.

not strictly speaking a holiday resort since it lacks a beach, it is nevertheless a popular base for sightseeing.

The city contains few vestiges of its rich past, owing to a great fire that destroyed much of it in 1922. However, there are still many places of interest well worth visiting.

If you leave from Cumhuriyet Meydani (Republic Square), where there is an imposing statue of Ataturk, you can walk along Ataturk Caddesi, which runs along the seafront and is lined with restaurants, night-clubs and travel agencies. At Konak Meydani there is an elegant clock-tower in the

Hotels and Restaurants
Particularly recommended are the **Buyuk Efes**, expensive by Turkish standards, but worth the extra; and the **Etap Izmir Hotel**. There are many restaurants on the waterfront, the **Deniz** being one of the best.

Tourism Bureau: G.O.P. Bulv. Buyuk Efes Otel Alti, 1/C (tel: (51) 142127), telex 53451.

Excursions

Izmir is an ideal point of
departure for many excursions,
including trips to the historic
sites of Ephesus and
Aphrodisias.

KUSADASI

In the centre of Turkey's Aegean
coast, in the region of ancient
Ionia, lies Kusadasi, the 'Island of
Birds', surrounded by some of
the richest historical sites in the
world.

Kusadasi's superb setting,
pleasant beaches, colourful
harbour and marina, pavement
cafés, quayside restaurants and
wide variety of shops have made
the resort one of the Turkish
Aegean's most popular holiday
spots, although it was included in
the Aegean itineraries of cruise
ships long before the Turkish
tourism boom started in earnest.
Indeed, such is the popularity of
this port town, with its easy
access to the ruined city of
Ephesus—a 'must' on any
visitor's itinerary—that as many
as eight ships a day call here
during the high season.

Despite considerable
development and expansion in
recent years the resort, which is
opposite the Greek island of
Samos, has managed to hold on
to a great deal of its charm.

Beaches

Kusadasi has two beaches: the
none-too-inspiring town beach,
and a much nicer one known as
Kadinlar, or Ladies' Beach, about
2 miles (3km) from the harbour
area. Here, fine powder sand
stretches for about half a mile,
and is well served by *lokantas*
and restaurants that back the

beach. However, for the serious
sunbather who cannot even
contemplate being in the shade,
there are also roving Turks
offering anything from corn on
the cob right through to chilled
beer and soft drinks. Some of the
better beaches in and around
Kusadasi are owned by hotel
complexes, but the modest
entrance fee is redeemable
against drinks and snacks.

The wide, clean promenade
which separates the sea from the
main avenue is a good spot for a
pre-dinner or early morning
stroll, while the resort's
numerous attractions include an
old caravanserai—where the
camel trains and merchants
stopped overnight—which is
now a stylish hotel with an
attractive if relatively expensive
courtyard restaurant.

Shopping

There are shady terraces
throughout Kusadasi where one
can sit and sip *raki* or a glass of
sweet Turkish tea. The main
street is lined with little shops
offering tempting bargains—
anything and everything,
including leatherware,
jewellery, brass, copper and
onyx, as well as inexpensive tee-
shirts.

Attractions

Kusadasi's old quarter is a
picturesque and atmospheric
maze of winding streets, some
rising steeply above the
harbour, with houses adorned
with colourful flowers and bird-
cages. In the lower street, just
behind the seafront, are the
majority of the shops.

On the little isle known as
Guvercin Adasi (Isle of Doves),

which is joined to the mainland by a small jetty, is a fortress built by the Turks in the 14th or 15th century and said to have been a den of notorious pirates whose daring escapades were known throughout the Mediterranean. Today, the surrounding gardens, and the discothèque inside the castle, are the popular haunts of holiday-makers, especially in the evenings when the sun is setting and the whole bay takes on a magical quality and atmosphere.

Hotels and Restaurants

Recommended hotels include the **Kismet**, situated on a headland about 2 miles (3km) from the centre of town, with lovely gardens; **Club Caravanserai**, converted from the magnificent caravanserai built in 1618; and the **Tusan Hotel**, on the outskirts. At the other end of the scale, the **Diamond Pension** is a delightful, simply furnished small hotel for those on a budget looking for a quiet location by the water's edge.

As well as a Turkish night held at the Caravanserai, complete with traditional Turkish food and belly dancing, there are literally hundreds of *lokantas* and restaurants, including one Chinese. If you want to find a good bar, look upward— Kusadasi has more than its fair share of roofbars.

The restaurants and bars at Kadinlar range from the thatched roof and fishing net variety with rickety tables, to smarter establishments such as the **Salmuk** which puts on live music.

The old 17th-century caravanserai in Kusadasi has been converted into a luxury hotel

Kusadasi is also rich in discos and many of the restaurants also have live music at least one day of the week—a blessing or a curse depending on your point of view.

Tourism Bureau: Iskele Meyd. (tel: (6361) 1103). By the Customs Office at the landing stage.

Gulf of Kusadasi

Guzelcamli

The great sweep of the landlocked Gulf of Kusadasi is broken up by small promontories into several bays fringed by long sandy beaches. And in one of these bays, about 16 miles (25.5km) from the centre of Kusadasi, nestles the small, unsophisticated but fast-developing resort of Guzelcamli. Guzelcamli is a good choice for those looking for a relaxing, laid-back beach holiday with the bonus of Kusadasi's big-resort attractions only a short and inexpensive *dolmus* taxi ride away. The resort, as yet unspoilt and typically Turkish, has sprung up round a pretty bay and its beach of coarse sand.

The old village, set a short distance from the beach, offers a range of small *lokantas*, bars and restaurants, and it is here that the *dolmus* taxis pick up passengers seeking the diversions of Kusadasi.

Beaches

In addition to the resort's own beaches, there is another, more pleasant beach within walking distance, equipped with loungers and shades and also a beach bar. There are also two more delightful beaches within the nearby national park, famous for its natural beauty and its delightful, uncrowded and unpolluted coves and beaches. All these beaches can be reached quite easily by *dolmus* taxi.

Excursions from Kusadasi

Even those with little interest in history should not miss the opportunity of making an excursion to the magnificent ruins of Ephesus about half an hour from Kusadasi, and one of Turkey's most impressive ancient sites. Most people reach Ephesus by joining one of the numerous excursions from Kusadasi; but it's just as easy by *dolmus* taxi—the journey is about 7 miles (11km). In addition, there are excursions to the fascinating old Ionian cities of Priene and Miletus, while throughout the summer regular boat trips operate from Kusadasi to the Greek island of Samos.

♦♦♦
EPHESUS

Travellers who visited Ephesus in the early 19th century found nothing but a few cottages, and

Ephesus – the almost-complete theatre in a theatrical setting

did not make even a passing reference to the place in their notes. Yet today, it is among the most famous historic sites in Turkey, and the most visited. The first excavations were undertaken in 1896 by Austrian archaeologists, and have continued virtually uninterrupted since.

It is one of three cities planned by the architect Hippodamos, who lived in Miletus in the 4th century BC: the plan applied in Miletus was used subsequently in Ephesus and Priene. Known by some as the grid plan, it consists of intercrossing streets, the main roads lined by public buildings and temples, and the minor roads by private houses. From a vantage point on a hillside behind the city, the grid system of streets is clearly visible.

The three main roads are the Harbour Road or Arcadius, the Marble Road and Curette Road. Most of the buildings visible today are ranged along these three roads, and almost all date from the Roman period.

On entering the city from the direction of the harbour the first building to strike the eye is the splendid amphitheatre on the slope of Panayir Mountain. With a seating capacity of 24,000, this is the largest theatre in Anatolia. Originally built in the Hellenistic period, it was extensively altered by the Romans, and during Byzantine times much of the seating was removed and the stone used in other buildings. Many of these have been recovered by archaeologists and the theatre today appears much as it did in Roman times.

At the junction of Marble Road and Curette Road, the façade of the Celsus Library, one of the finest examples of Roman period decoration, acts like a magnet. The building faces east so that the morning light entered the windows of the reading rooms. It was built by a rich Roman named Hulius Aquila in memory of his father Celsus, a prefect of Asia, and its collection of books was one of the largest in the ancient world.

Further along Curette Road to the right can be seen the tiled houses of rich Ephesians, rising by stages on vaults and built in the form of a peristyle around a colonnaded courtyard. The ivory objects, valuable statuettes and frescos discovered when excavating these houses confirm that they were the homes of the rich and powerful. The brick pillars under the floors show that they had under-floor heating in the manner of Roman baths.

Of the famous Temple of Artemis, once one of the Seven Wonders of the Ancient World, unfortunately nothing but a single column remains. A Grecianised version of the far more ancient Anatolian goddess Cybele, the goddess of fertility, Artemis was worshipped in all Greek cities, but in Ephesus her importance was far more wide-ranging. The statue of Artemis in the Temple was believed to have been the gift of the Amazons or, according to another version of the story, to have come from heaven.

Not only did Artemis of Ephesus bring prosperity to the region but, the residents believed, she cured the sick, was a regulator of

THE AEGEAN COAST

commercial life, overcame difficulties, and protected the city from danger.

Such a generous goddess obviously deserved extra special treatment in return, and a large retinue of priests, priestesses, temple virgins, attendants who dressed the statue of Artemis and musicians served at the Temple.

◆◆◆
SELCUK

The town of Selcuk, which lies just outside Ephesus, is dominated by a Byzantine fortress, once the largest temple in Asia Minor, surrounded by 129 marble columns, and also has a museum with interesting objects recovered from Ephesus, including a life-size figure of Artemis.

◆◆
HOUSE OF THE VIRGIN MARY

On a site 4¼ miles (7km) above Selcuk, now occupied by a small chapel, the Virgin Mary is said to have spent the last few years of her life. The site is now a place of pilgrimage.

Tourism bureau: Ataturk Mah. Efes Muzesi Karsisi 23, Selcuk (tel: (5451) 1328 or 1945). Opposite the museum.

PRIENE

Priene, perched high on a rock and now separated from the sea by 10 miles (16km) of alluvial plain, was one of the busiest ports of the Ionian Federation. What makes the site of particular interest is the system of geometric planning introduced in the 4th century BC by Hippodamos of Miletus. The theatre is the most interesting of

Priene's remains; the lower tiers are virtually intact, and the whole theatre retains its original character. Only a few columns remain of the Temple of Athena, which was a classic example of Ionian architecture. Priene is about 30 miles (50km) south of Kusadasi.

◆◆
MILETUS

Miletus, like Priene, was once a great Ionian port, with no fewer than four harbours, and the native city of several philosophers and sages. Most of the monuments at the site are badly ruined except for the theatre and the Baths of Faustina. The theatre, reconstructed during the Roman period, is an impressive building. Five columns of the once great Temple of Athena have been re-erected to give an indication of its original massive scale. Miletus is about 30 miles (50km) south of Kusadasi.
End of excursions

◆◆◆
MARMARIS

With its dramatic setting at the foot of pine-clad hills among some of Turkey's most staggeringly beautiful scenery, a relaxing atmosphere and excellent facilities and amenities, the picturesque, palm-filled resort of Marmaris is one of the most popular in the whole of Turkey. It is even a favourite holiday haunt of the Turks themselves and, although its beach is nothing special, its popularity is not difficult to understand. The lovely fjord-like stretch of coastline where the Aegean meets the

An enterprising old gentleman and his weighing machine, Marmaris

Mediterranean offers numerous unspoilt and practically deserted coves fringing a warm, turquoise-blue sea, making the area a good choice for those who enjoy sunbathing and seawater swimming.

Once the ancient port of Physcus, occupying an important place on the commercial trading route between Anatolia, Rhodes and Egypt, Marmaris was part of the southwest Aegean kingdom of Caria, the two most powerful cities of which were Knidos and the capital, Bodrum. In the 6th century BC Caria fell to the Lydians and was then subjugated by the Persians until Alexander the Great ousted them in 334BC. The Romans had conquered the region by 163BC, and after the division of the Roman Empire, the area fell under Byzantine rule. The region was wrested from the Byzantines in AD1282 by the Turkish Emir of Mentese, and in 1425 the rule of the Ottoman Turks was established.

Today, Marmaris is a well-equipped holiday resort with scores of excellent hotels and holiday villages, many of international standard, as well as numerous simpler but well-furnished and equipped smaller hotels, family-owned-and-managed *pensions*, and modern villas and apartments.

Dominating the scene is a medieval castle built by Sultan Suleyman the Magnificent on a hill behind the yacht harbour. In addition to its historic battlements, it offers great views of the town and the bay beyond.

Beaches

The best beaches are not in the resort itself, but further along the bay, all easily accessible by *dolmus* taxi. Best of all are those reached by boat: beautiful, practically deserted sandy coves popular for picnics or lazy days enjoying the sun, the sea and the lovely setting. There is an impressive range of facilities for watersports lovers, with sailing, windsurfing and water-skiing all readily and inexpensively available, together with the latest craze, jet-skiing.

Boat *dolmus*, the water-borne equivalents of the taxis, go to the many beaches and islets round the bay, while regular ferry services operate to Rhodes, or you can join one of the main excursion programmes available.

THE AEGEAN COAST

The harbour and marina area are particularly lively and colourful, teeming with fishing boats, excursion craft and elegant yachts, while the attractive palm-fringed seafront promenade has seats placed at regular intervals so you can sit and admire the beautiful bay or enjoy a cool drink or an ice cream from one of several kiosks.

Shopping
The principal shops—Marmaris is arguably the most attractive of Turkey's holiday resorts for shopping—are located in the streets leading off the seafront promenade, and offer a good selection of goods and crafts. Many of them remain open well into the evening. Especially popular take-home gifts are jars of local honey, and sponges.

Hotels and Restaurants
Marmaris has an excellent range of quality hotels, *pensions* and self-catering accommodation. Recommended are the **Karacan**, a well-furnished and well-equipped hotel superbly situated right by the beach; the **Lidya**, one of the best-located hotels in the resort, set amid lovely tropical gardens; and the **Flamingo**, which has a large shady terrace restaurant leading to a sunbathing terrace and the beach.
There is also a good choice of restaurants, as well as pastry shops with their enticing wares, bars—one of the most popular is the Daily News—and several lively discos.
Tourism bureau: Iskele Meyd. 39 (tel: (6121) 1035). Next to the Customs Office at the harbour.

Icmeler
As Marmaris becomes more popular, Icmeler, some 10 minutes away by taxi, is developing into a resort in its own right thanks to an attractive bronze sandy beach stretching for about half a mile. The sea here is warm, clear and pollution-free, making the resort particularly popular with swimmers and those who enjoy windsurfing. Board-sailing and watersports equipment, including jet-skis, are readily available for hire, as are beach loungers and sunshades. Although it is becoming increasingly popular, Icmeler has retained much of its unspoilt small-resort appeal, and is a favourite with holiday-makers looking for a quieter, relaxing and unsophisticated beach holiday amidst delightful scenery.
The village itself offers a selection of small general stores, fruit and vegetable stalls, bars and *lokantas*, and a choice of simple, ethnic restaurants. There is even a discothèque whose popularity is such that it attracts holiday-makers and residents from its much bigger and much more sophisticated near neighbour Marmaris.

Excursions from Marmaris
As a base for sightseeing, either by water or road, Marmaris is well situated. Treasures such as the ancient Lycian tombs carved into the rock face at Fethiye and the sun-worshipper's paradise of Olu Deniz, with its white sandy beaches and inviting sea, are both within fairly easy reach, as are Pamukkale, and the ancient

site of Aphrodisias.

Islands: A pleasant day out can also be enjoyed on Paradise Island, totally uncommercialised except for one simple *lokanta*, while excursions regularly operate to Cleopatra's Island, whose silver sand is said to have been specially imported by Mark Antony from Turkey's Black Sea region.

◆◆◆
PAMUKKALE

Pamukkale is one of the many jewels in the Turkish tourism crown. The word actually means 'cotton castle', a fitting description for an extraordinary site where the waters of thermal springs laden with calcium oxide have formed a dazzling white petrified cascade of stalactites, flowing over the plateau's edge into a series of basins and pools. It is best reached by bus or train to Denizli, then *dolmus* taxi for about 10½ miles (17km).

◆◆◆
HIERAPOLIS

On top of the plateau are the ruins of ancient Hierapolis, founded in the 2nd century BC and among whose ancient buildings are the thermal baths, part of which now form a museum of sculpture. The site also includes a Christian basilica, Temple of Apollo, theatre and Martyrium of Philip, dedicated to the Apostle who was martyred here in AD80.

At night at Pamukkale the pools of water overflow into each other down the cliffs, adding more calcium to the enormous stalactites that fringe them

◆◆◆
APHRODISIAS

The ruins of Aphrodisias form one of the most important and attractive archaeological sites in Turkey, situated as they are at the foot of the impressive Baba Dag Mountains.

The city was the centre of the cult of Aphrodite and possessed a flourishing school of sculpture, but it reached the zenith of its prosperity as a religious, artistic and literary centre during the Roman period. Aphrodisias' huge stadium, which could accommodate 30,000 spectators, is one of the best preserved in the Roman world. Fourteen elegant columns remain standing of the Temple of Aphrodite, which was a pilgrimage centre and a place of sanctuary. Near the Temple is a beautiful gateway, and there is also a small odeon or concert hall, with sunken orchestra and a stage elaborately decorated with mosaics and statuary. Several Ionic porticos and 12 columns remain of the agora or marketplace. Also of interest are the thermal baths of Hadrian and two palatial residences that belonged to a bishop and a Byzantine official. Don't miss the fine sculptures displayed in the museum in nearby Geyre.
End of excursions

◆◆◆
OLU DENIZ

Olu Deniz offers one of the most spectacular and beautiful beaches in the whole of Turkey, with a magnificent crescent of dazzling pale sand fringing a clear, pollution-free lagoon of turquoise blue. Set in an area of

With a setting like this, no wonder Olu Deniz is a favourite holiday spot

outstanding natural beauty—to the extent of being declared a nature park—the lagoon is almost entirely cut off from the sea but for a narrow channel, making it perfect for safe swimming and watersports. Located about 10 miles (16km) from the ancient port/resort of Fethiye, Olu Deniz—the name literally means 'Dead Sea'— boasts a staggeringly beautiful picture-postcard setting where, mercifully, tourist development has been severely restricted. The main beach at Olu Deniz is a great sweep of silver sand, fronted by a few bars and

beach. A small charge is made to enter this area in order that litter bins can be provided and the place kept clean and tidy.

Hotels

Apart from the **Meri Hotel**, which virtually has Olu Deniz to itself and whose standards vary enormously, most of the holiday accommodation is located a few miles inland in the tiny villages of Ovacik and Hisaronu, leaving the beach area around Olu Deniz delightfully unspoilt.

Ovacik is about a five minute journey by *dolmus* taxi from Olu Deniz, and is an attractive little development of small *pensions*, hotels and *lokantas* magnificently set in delightful countryside.

Hisaronu, likewise, is only a few miles from Olu Deniz, and is also surrounded by lush green countryside and fruit orchards. It boasts one of the area's most pleasant hotels, the Hotel Holiday, whose facilities include a large swimming pool with terrace and bar, as well as a second, smaller pool.

Those looking for something really different in the way of accommodation may care to consider the obscure but picturesque village of **Ocakkoy**, which lies between Olu Deniz and Fethiye. A twisting track leads through a pine forest to this small settlement of stone houses built on the slopes of a hill and surrounded by pine woods. The village, abandoned by the Greeks some 60 years ago, comprises a selection of one-bedroom houses, furnished with antiques, richly patterned rugs and *kilims*, and with modern

lokantas that offer excellent variety at ridiculously low prices. At one end of the bay a thickly wooded peninsula forms one arm of the lagoon, with a very narrow throat open to the sea. The landward side of the lagoon has a beach of fine golden sand. There are delightful boat trips to deserted islands and to a fascinating fish farm, or you can join in one of the beach barbecues that are a feature of this resort.

The countryside around Olu Deniz is also well worth exploring. There is even a delightful area set within the nature park that is equipped with tables and chairs in the woods that run down to the

THE AEGEAN COAST

bathrooms. Owned by a Turkish sea-captain and his English wife, the village also has a small restaurant, outdoor bar, swimming pool, tennis court and a pottery, and enjoys a magnificent view over the valley. The owners run a daily mini-bus shuttle service down to the beach at Olu Deniz.

Restaurants
There are several restaurants and bars near the beach at Olu Deniz, and even a couple of small discos, or you could head off to the stylish and sophisticated new restaurant built on the very edge of the cliffs that form Olu Deniz Bay. There is also a reasonable choice of hotel restaurants and bars in both Ovacik and Hisaronu, as well as small *lokantas*, while the bright lights of Fethiye, with its shops and more sophisticated tourist amenities, are only a short *dolmus* drive away.

HOW TO GET TO THE AEGEAN

By Air
Holiday resorts on the Turkish Aegean coast are served by two principal airports, Izmir and Dalaman, although a new domestic airport is planned for Bodrum to which there will be flights from Istanbul.

Izmir Airport is served by direct scheduled services from many European cities and also by charter flights. At the airport, coaches transfer beach holiday-makers to their chosen resort. Several of these are easily reached from Izmir, including Foca, to the northwest, Cesme,

due west, and Kusadasi. Holiday-makers on self-drive arrangements can pick up their cars at the airport or at their overnight hotel. Likewise, many coach tours around Turkey have Izmir as the starting point.

Dalaman Airport first opened for charter flights in 1982 and has since been extended to cope with the increasing number of flights here from major European cities. There is a 24-hour taxi service available at the airport, as well as car rental facilities. Approximate distances by road to some of the nearest resorts are: Dalyan 19 miles (30km), Fethiye 39 miles (63km), Marmaris 65 miles (105km) and Bodrum 132 miles (213km). Coach services operate from Dalaman Town to Marmaris, between 07.00 and 18.15hrs (75 minutes); Bodrum at 11.00 and 13.30hrs (3 hours); and Fethiye, hourly or more frequently during the peak holiday period (1 hour).

By Boat
Turkish Maritime Lines boats leave Istanbul regularly, stopping at ports along the Aegean coast. There are also frequent services to Izmir from Marseilles and Genoa, and car-ferry links in the summer from Venice and Brindisi.

By road
The car journey across Europe is long, sometimes tedious and, in parts, not at all easy. Motorists travelling from the main centres of western Europe can remove up to 500 miles (800km) from their journey by using the Greek port of Piraeus and taking a car ferry from there to the Turkish Aegean ports.

THE MEDITERRANEAN

Known as the Turkish Riviera, or the Turquoise Coast, the Mediterranean region of Turkey has much to offer the holiday-maker, including a delightful climate even in the winter months, long stretches of fine, sandy beach, excellent hotels, a good range of sightseeing options and plenty of value-for-money restaurants.

The whole coast is rich in legend and history, with many ruins of ancient cities, theatres and great Crusader castles. Tourist Office literature boasts that Mark Antony once gave part of these shores to Cleopatra as a wedding gift, and whether the legend is true or not, there can be no denying that the shoreline is exceedingly attractive, with seemingly endless stretches of white sand set against the often snow-capped peaks of the Taurus Mountains.

The verdant shores are covered with pine forests, orange groves and banana plantations, splashed here and there with the vivid pink of wild oleanders, as well as mushrooming hotels and holiday villages.

The principal resorts are Antalya, magnificently situated on the shores of a broad bay; Side, located between two vast stretches of sandy beach next to the ruins of an ancient city; Kemer, a 20-mile stretch of sand/pebble beach among pine woods and citrus groves; Mersin; Antakya (ancient Antioch), once one of the greatest cities of the world; and the small but fast-developing fishing ports of Kas and Kalkan.

The popularity of the quiet and lovely village of Kalkan, with its sheltered harbour, is growing each year

THE MEDITERRANEAN COAST

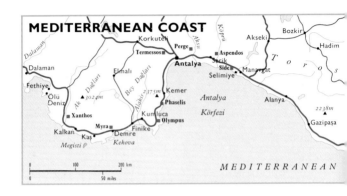

MEDITERRANEAN COAST

♦♦♦
ALANYA

The lively and popular holiday resort of Alanya lies on a delightful stretch of coast on the 'Turkish Riviera', and is sheltered by densely wooded, purple-tinged hills. Two sweeping, sandy bays curve round the headland, where a giant peninsula juts out dramatically into the sea. Known in ancient times as Korakesion, it was founded in the 4th century BC and, during Roman times, was a notorious pirate stronghold. The town was later annexed by Alaeddin Keykubat, who made it both his winter residence and his naval base.

From the lower town a road winds round the harbour, with its interesting arched boatyards and medieval Red Tower, and leads up to the old Seljuk fortress, which keeps watch over Alanya from its impressive rocky perch. The ruins here command superb views across the bay to the distant snow-capped peaks of the Taurus Mountains.

Alanya itself is a labyrinth of shops, bars and restaurants. A highlight for many visitors is its weekly market, when the stalls spill over with local produce and livestock jostles with the crowd.

Fortress

The well-preserved, double-walled Seljuk fortress of Alanya has 150 towers still standing, and contains mosques, a Byzantine church, a covered bazaar, caravanserai and cisterns. The outer wall is 5 miles (8 km) long and took 12 years to build, while the existence of some 400 cisterns made it possible to store sufficient water to withstand any length of siege. Of particular interest to visitors are a high ceilinged room topped by a vast dome and the remains of the *bedesten* (a domed store), which once boasted 26 rooms and vast storage spaces.

Red Tower

The Red Tower, or Kizil Kule, which reinforces the low wall of the fortress at the junction of the north and east walls, served as a watchtower, and was built in

THE MEDITERRANEAN COAST

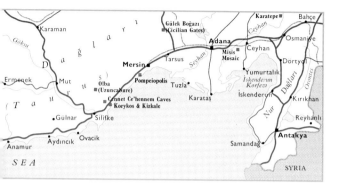

1225 after the model of the Crusaders' castles. It has been skilfully restored. The first two storeys are made of reddish stone blocks, and the two upper ones are built from huge red bricks.

Shipyard
The 13th-century shipyard, whose entrance is flanked by a guardroom on the left and a mosque on the right, consisted of five compartments; its foundations were hewn out of the rock. Turkish warships were built here from timber brought from the Taurus Mountains.

Damlatas Cave
At the foot of the promontory on the eastern side is the Damlatas Cave, thought to be anything up to about 15,000 years old. This boasts wonderful multi-coloured stalagmites and stalactites, and its high humidity is reputed to benefit sufferers from asthma and other respiratory complaints. One of the stalagmites is said to resemble a human form, and is identified with the Virgin Mary.

Boat Trips
Alanya is one of Turkey's major ports of entry, and the harbour has been extended to accommodate a great number of ships and boats, many of which leave regularly to cruise along the surrounding shores which abound in caves and inlets. Of special interest are the Blue Grotto, with its phosphorescent rocks, and Maidens' Cave, where pirates used to keep their female captives.

Sports
Alanya offers good watersports, with waterskiing and windsurfing available at various hotels. There are pedalos and boats for hire, and lots of opportunities for swimming and snorkelling, tennis and table tennis.

Hotels and Restaurants
Alanya boasts numerous international-standard hotels, and many more are under construction. One of the best of the existing hotels is the **Alantur**, located alongside a lovely stretch of beach, with a

wide range of facilities that include no fewer than three swimming pools.

The resort offers numerous good restaurants serving tasty Turkish specialities, and plenty of bars, cafés and discos. For dancing of a more exotic nature, the hotels' ethnic evenings, with the accent on audience participation, are a good opportunity for some unusual photographs.

Tourism bureau: Carsi Mah, Kalearkasi Cad (tel: (3231) 1240). Opposite the museum, near the Damlatas Cave.

Excursions from Alanya

The road east of Alanya, through the village of Gazipasa, leads to what is often claimed, and with some justification, to be the most beautiful stretch of coastline in Turkey. The road itself clings to the pine-clad mountain slopes which plunge steeply down to the sea, offering spectacular views of cliffs, coves and the brilliant turquoise waters of the Mediterranean.

Just outside Anamur, 80 miles (128km) from Alanya, are the ruins of ancient Anemorium, with its double ramparts, a theatre, odeon and a necropolis. A fine, well-preserved Crusader castle is nearby, set between two curving, sandy beaches, and from the top of the fort there is a splendid view of the surrounding countryside and coast.

East of Anamur the road rises and falls until you reach the Plain of Silifke. Just before Silifke is the little resort of Tasucu, with its sandy beach and harbour from where regular boat services operate to Cyprus.

Located slightly inland is

Silifke itself, 136 miles (217km) beyond Anamur, set at the foot of a fortress crowning the hill that was the acropolis of ancient Seleucia and Calycadnos. In the town is an old bridge crossing the Calycadnos River, today called the Goksu, and the remains of a Roman theatre, temple and necropolis.

Just beyond Silifke at Narlikuyu is a Roman mosaic depicting the Three Graces. Further along are the deep chasms known as Heaven and Hell; Heaven contains the ruins of a 5th-century chapel. Nearby is a deep cave full of stalactites and stalagmites.

◆◆◆
ANTAKYA

Antakya—known as Antioch in ancient times—is pleasantly situated in a fertile plain surrounded by grand mountains, and was once the prosperous and ostentatious capital of the Seleucid kings, who were notorious for their indulgent lifestyles. In Roman times the city was a great centre of artistic, scientific and commercial activity. It was also a centre of Christianity, where St Barnabus, St Paul and St Peter all stayed and preached. Traces left by successive occupants of Antioch go back as far as the 4th millennium BC. The town was founded by one of Alexander's generals and was constantly enlarged by subsequent Seleucids, while under the Romans it became the third city of the empire, with 500,000 inhabitants. It was full of theatres, baths, canals and markets, and even had street lighting.

Museum

Most of what has been preserved of the ancient glory is now in the Hatay Archaeological Museum. In addition to items from the various excavations in the surrounding area, it also contains a collection of 2nd- and 3rd-century Roman mosaics, most of which once adorned the luxury villas in the vale 5 miles (8km) to the south.

A little outside the town is the Grotto of St Peter, the cave church from which St Peter is said to have preached for the first time and so founded the Christian community.

◆◆◆
ANTALYA

Antalya is a thriving, increasingly sophisticated town noted for its shady, palm-fringed boulevards, picturesque old quarters and attractive, newly-restored harbour.

The town is splendidly spread over a cliff promontory between the beaches of Konyaalti and Lara, with mountains forming a dramatic backdrop. Eastward stretches a beautiful length of coastline indented with many streams, with waterfalls cascading down into the sea from the heights of the adjacent cliffs, while the area is further blessed with shady forests, lakes, and one of the world's most pleasant climates.

The town offers a great many diversions for the holiday-maker, as well as being an excellent base for excursions to local beauty spots, and for visits to the ancient sites and spacious beaches in the vicinity.

Founded by Greek settlers in

Valuable items in the Hatay Museum on Gunduz Caddesi include this mosaic from a villa in Roman Antioch

about 1000BC, it was named Attaleia by Attalus II of Pergamon who, foiled in his attempt to take Side, established a naval base here. Known as Satalia to the Crusaders who used the port to avoid Seljuk territory, it was renamed Antalya in the 13th century.

Its principal attractions, which can be visited either on foot or by horse-drawn carriage, include well-preserved city ramparts and the monumental three-arched Hadrian's Gate, in decorated marble, which was built in AD130 to commemorate the emperor's visit to the city. At the edge of the attractive municipal park—a favourite place for promenades amidst a variety of exotic flowers—is the Hidirlik Kulesi, which was formerly a lighthouse.

Harbour

The narrow winding streets of the old quarter, lined with pretty

THE MEDITERRANEAN COAST

wooden houses, lead to the bustling harbour, where cruise ships regularly call. The harbour has been extensively restored and refurbished in recent years, and is now an attractive, lively area complete with open-air restaurants, terraced bars, souvenir shops and promenades. Declared a conservation area in 1972, the narrow streets of traditional houses leading down to the harbour are enjoying a new lease of life, many as attractive small bars or restaurants, or even guesthouses. Those with courtyards often display locally-made carpets and woven rugs.

Archaeological museum
On the Konyaalti Road, at the western edge of the town, is an archaeological museum that houses a rich collection of ceramics, mosaics and figurines recovered from the surrounding areas. Many of the exhibits are placed outside in a pleasant garden that affords views across Antalya Bay. An ethnographic section features a display of the nomadic life, with fully furnished tents and photographs of camels laden with camping equipment and household goods.

Shopping
The town is also good for shopping, with a colourful market and a wide selection of shops and boutiques, many selling good quality clothing at very reasonable prices.

Beaches
There are two main beaches on either side of Antalya. On the western edge is the huge crescent of the shingle and

The restored, protected harbour is the focal point of Antalya

pebble Konyaalti Beach, and to the east the long sandy Lara Beach. The latter is much the better of the two, and almost a resort in its own right, with several international-standard hotels already in existence and many more being built.

Hotels and Restaurants
Antalya is the setting for one of the best hotels in Turkey, the stylish and luxurious **Talya Hotel**, situated on the cliff top. Candlelit dinners by the outdoor swimming pool are a feature. The elegant **Adalya Hotel**, adjacent to the newly restored harbour is also recommended.
Tourism bureau: Selcuk Mah, Ahi Yusuf Cami Yani, Mermerli Kaleici (tel: (311) 15271/11326).

Excursions from Antalya
Antalya is an excellent base for
exploring ancient sites.
Southwest takes you through the
Bey Daglari National Park to
Phaselis, while north is the road
to Termessos. To the east are
Perge, Aspendos and Side.

PERGE
The ancient site of Perge, which
lies less than 15 miles (24km)
east of Antalya, contains much to
interest the visitor, not least an
impressive theatre and equally
impressive stadium. Until the
time of Alexander the Great,
Perge was an independent city
republic; it then became a
principal city of Pamphylia in
Hellenistic times. The city
prospered under Rome, its
importance not declining until
the Byzantine period.

Just outside the city walls is a
Greco-Roman stadium which
could seat an audience of 25,000.
The auditorium has a
colonnaded gallery running
round the top which was built
against a hillside. Adjacent to the
stadium is one of the biggest and
best-preserved theatres of
antiquity, which could seat
approximately 15,000.
You enter the Hellenistic
enclosure through a Roman gate,
behind which lies a triumphal
arch that has been restored by
archaeologists. Further along is
the handsome older city gate,
dating from the 3rd century BC,
which is flanked by two lofty
round towers and contains a
horseshoe-shaped court. This
gate leads on to a long
colonnaded way that was once
lined with shops and mosaic
pavements. Opposite the ruins of
the large agora stands a building
which used to house the thermal
baths and gymnasium.

◆◆◆
TERMESSOS
The romantic ruins of the ancient
city fortress of Termessos are
perched on a craggy peak about
21¾ miles (35km) from Antalya.
In ancient times this mountain
area was known as Pisidia, and
Termessos was its most powerful
city. The ruins are set within a
profusion of wild flowers, olive
trees and mountain pine, making
it one of the most beautiful
ancient sites in Turkey.
The city was founded by a war-
like, courageous people who put
up a successful resistance to
Alexander the Great, forcing him
to raise his siege and retreat in
frustration. He took his revenge

by burning the olive groves around the town. Towards the end of the 3rd century AD the population of the town decreased, its fortunes began to decline, and in the 5th century it was abandoned altogether. The entrance portal to the city is the monumental Hadrian's Gate. After passing through you come to the traces of a still unexcavated gymnasium to the left, and beyond this is a small theatre which once seated 4,200 people, very few in comparison with the theatres of Pamphylia. The odeon's walls, up to 10m in height, still stand. This sturdy building was originally tiled, and traces of windows are to be seen on the eastern and western walls. The interior was probably faced with marble. To the south of the odeon lies the Temple of Artemis, built in Roman times by the wife of the sculptor who made the temple statue. Next to this is another small Roman-period temple set on a podium, the Temple of Zeus, who was the patron god of Termessos. Here reliefs depict a battle between gods and monsters.

ASPENDOS

Aspendos, just over 30 miles (48km) from Antalya, is also known as Belkis, after the modern village of Belkis which is near by. Although it may be said that it was founded as a colony of Argos, in fact it is known to have existed well before.

Visitors are immediately confronted with the high outer walls of the theatre, set against the eastern slopes of a small hill and pierced with windows. The high entrance wall impresses, even without the fine works of art which once adorned it. The theatre is still in use today during the annual festival of Antalya, and is capable of seating 20,000 spectators. It was built during

This bridge in Aspendos is from the time of the Seljuk Turks; some believe the city itself dates from as early as 1180BC

the 2nd century BC during the reign of Antoninus.

Apart from the magnificent theatre, other constructions of note on or near the site include the impressive aqueducts and the stadium. The aqueducts have survived sufficiently in several places to show how magnificently designed were the water systems of the ancient city. You can trace these aqueducts by following the road around the village for ½ mile (1km), and on foot from the site by following the footpath around the walls of the acropolis before reaching the stadium, which has a rock tomb to the right and a small sarcophagus to the left.

Waterfalls
Other popular excursions from Antalya are to the spectacular Duden Waterfalls which plunge over the cliff edge to the sea. Further up the same river are the equally spectacular Upper Duden Waterfalls.
End of excursions

♦♦♦
KALKAN
Overlooking an attractive harbour, this picturesque fishing village is becoming an increasingly popular resort, thanks to its setting, excellent restaurants and friendly atmosphere. Predominantly a fishing hamlet with a tranquil, sleepy air, its quaint old houses, with wooden balconies overhanging the road, tumble down to the sea. Its narrow streets, some of which are cobbled, house a couple of general stores, a stall selling exotic fruit and vegetables, and a few souvenir shops.

Boats leave the harbour most mornings to ferry visitors to nearby beaches and small bays, although it is possible to swim from jetties down on the small pebbly area on the harbour front. Less than 4 miles (6.4km) east of Kalkan lies Kaputas, a beach of white sand with turquoise waters.

Hotels and Restaurants
Kalkan is developing fast, but of the smaller, older-style hotels and *pensions* there, **Pasha's Inn** and the **Balikci Han** are two of the best, the former having a delightful rooftop terrace which commands views of the harbour and surrounding islets. There are several simple but pleasant bars and restaurants overlooking the harbour, all offering good value for money.

Excursions from Kalkan
Popular excursions are to the ancient site of Xanthos, and to Patara, 10 miles (16km) distant, which offers not only one of the finest beaches in Turkey, but also some fascinating ruins.

KAS
Nestling at the foot of the Taurus Mountains on the shores of a deep blue bay, this little fishing village has suddenly been 'discovered' by holiday-makers. Its setting is outstanding, encircling a crescent bay at the end of a verdant fjord, enclosed to the north by a long lizard-like peninsula and sheltered on its seaward side by the lovely Greek islet of Castelorizzo. Originally called Habesos or Habesa in the ancient Lycian tongue, Kas was subsequently

The beautiful rugs and carpets on sale in Kas make fine souvenirs of Turkey: they are surprisingly reasonable

known as Antiphellos, and is one of the oldest settlements in the region of Lycia, even though most of the ancient settlement is now covered by the modern village. The rock tombs northeast of the town date from the 4th century BC. On a rise between the open sea and the hill, which was probably the acropolis of Antiphellos, lies a rock tomb in the Doric order, where an inside frieze depicts two dozen dancing female figures. The acropolis was surrounded by a fortified wall, of which traces can be seen on the façade facing the island of Meis. To the west of Kas stands the ancient theatre, enjoying a remarkable panorama. Its 26 rows of seats look straight out from the hillside to the sea. Visitors do not come to Kas for the beaches—there are none, apart from a few small stony coves—but for the friendliness of the locals and the natural beauty of this traditional village. Swimming in the resort is mainly from rocky platforms in clear waters, or from the pebbly coves. However, you can take a *dolmus* to the sandy beach of Kaputas, on the coastal road to Kalkan, while the long expanse of sand at Patara, less than 30 miles (48km) away, makes for a great day out on the beach.

Hotels
The **Mimosa Hotel**, on the road leading into Kas, is one of the best in the area; also recommended are the **Derya**, opposite the Mimosa, and the **Likya**.
Tourism bureau: Cumhuriyet Meyd 6 (tel: (3226) 1238). On the main square by the harbour.

Excursions from Kas
Excursions are available to

Demre, which is associated with the original St Nicholas, or you can join a boat trip to Kekova, where the sunken ruins of Lycian settlements can be seen.

DEMRE

Some say that the original St Nicholas, or Father Christmas, came not from the wintry lands of snow and igloos but from Turkey. His actual birthplace, in fact, was the village of Patara, but it was at Demre that he served as bishop and here there is a tiny church which bears his name.

St Nicholas was Bishop of Demre, then called Myra, in the 5th century AD at the time of Emperor Constantine. Legend has it that when he was young his parents died, leaving him a fortune. Nicholas used the money to help others, especially young people; and he is said to have made anonymous gifts of gold to girls from families too poor to give them a dowry.

As the St Nicholas cult developed, memory of him faded in his original home town, and earlier this century the roofless basilica of St Nicholas was used as a substitute for a mosque. It was only in the last decade, with the expansion of tourism, that the Turkish authorities realised the potential of the building, and after several years of restoration the church was finally opened in 1981 as a shrine to the saint. Beside the church is a statue of Father Christmas as he is known throughout the world: bearded, robed, and trundling a sackful of presents behind him.

KEKOVA

The lizard-shaped isle of Kekova, which lies off shore between the ruins of Andriake and Aperlae, is hauntingly beautiful, with Lycian sarcophagi scattered along the shore and lying half-submerged in lovely coves.
End of excursions

KEMER

Tourism first came here when the older yacht marina was built and sailing people started to appear in the town looking for somewhere to eat and drink and places to buy provisions and souvenirs. Today, the resort's attractive and well designed new marina is attracting even more yachts, giving Kemer an atmosphere not unlike Puerto Banus in Spain, while holiday villages have also sprung up to satisfy the needs of landlubbers. There are two beaches at the resort. The best is of the sand-mixed-with-pebble variety and stretches round the bay from the marina. The town beach is pebble, with convenient *lokantas* and cafés. The best beach in the area, this time of sand, is located on the outskirts of Kemer, by the Pension Gul 2. Cars can be hired locally in Kemer, there are plenty of taxis and a good bus service, so getting around is no problem. The regional capital, Antalya, is an hour or so's drive away.

Hotels

Most of the accommodation in Kemer is in holiday village-style units. The **Club Mediterranée** and **Club Robinson** villages are particularly popular, as is the newer Milta complex. The **Hotel Dragos**, which has a central seafront position is also recommended. A new **Hotel Ramada** is making its presence felt.

Tourism bureau: Belediye Binasi (tel: (3214) 1466, 1495). Located near the harbour on the ground floor of the Town Hall.

Excursions from Kemer

PHASELIS

Phaselis is a ten minute drive away. Here, in beautiful countryside, are the magnificent remains of an ancient city, by the side of an attractive beach. As at Olympus, the setting and atmosphere of Phaselis are very rewarding. The ruins are still being excavated, and although not on the grandest scale, include an attractive walk through a paved market, theatre, aqueduct and temple.

Once a major port with three natural harbours, Phaselis was founded in the 7th century BC as a colony of Rhodes, possibly on an earlier site. It was ruled by the Persians after Darius conquered Anatolia, and later by Alexander the Great, whom the inhabitants admitted without a struggle. After the death of Alexander the city was ruled by the Egyptian Ptolemaic dynasty from 209BC to 197BC, returned to the Rhodians until 160BC and then became part of the Lycian confederacy under Roman rule. The city enjoyed a great deal of prosperity through all the periods of its history, especially under the Romans. Like Olympus, Phaselis was under constant threat from

pirates in the first century BC, and was even ruled for a period by the pirate Zeniketes, until he was defeated by the Romans. During the Byzantine period the city became a bishopric. The vulnerability of its harbours to pirate attack began its decline in the 3rd century AD, however, a process speeded up by successive Arab raids. By the time the Seljuks conquered the region in the 11th century, Phaselis had ceased to be a port of any note.

In the military harbour you can still see the remains of a pier which extended from the city walls around the promontory. The ruins in Phaselis are scattered among trees that stretch down to the beach, making them picturesque as well as interesting.

OLYMPUS

Located between Kemer and the village of Adras, tucked in a rugged mountain gorge on the coast of Lycia, lie the unexcavated, overgrown ruins of this once-great port city. Here, palm trees flourish next to pine trees, citrus fruit is abundant and vegetables are grown year-round. With its mild climate, natural defences and strategic location half-way between Rhodes and Cyprus, it is easy to see why this valley was settled; it is less easy to understand why it was abandoned.

Olympus enjoyed a brief existence during the Hellenistic period, being one of the foremost members of the Lycian confederacy. Coins were struck here in the 2nd century BC, and in

78BC the city became the base of the pirate Zeniketes. He was finally defeated by the Roman governor of Lycia, Publius Servilius Vatia, in a sea battle, and forced to flee. He took refuge in his fortress near Olympus but by accident set his house alight with a torch he carried and was burned to death.

Under Roman rule Olympus became extremely prosperous, since its harbours were ideal for trade, and in AD129, after Hadrian visited the city, it was renamed Hadrianopolis. Opramas, a rich citizen of the Lycian League, paid for the construction of many fine buildings in the 2nd century AD. Towards the end of this century Olympus fell into the hands of pirates once again, and was impoverished as a result. It was used by Venetian and Genoese pirates for a period, during which time the Genoese built a harbour wall. After the pirates were routed by the Ottoman fleet, the city was abandoned altogether.

Although small, it is a fascinating site, the ruins of the city being set along the banks of a shallow stream that runs up the middle of the gorge. On the south side of the stream the ancient town wraps above the cliffs overlooking the sea and stretches more than a mile inland. There, among the fallen leaves, marble columns and a small Roman theatre, anonymous intact walls and elevated moss-covered floors fill the flat ground near the stream bed. Roman and Byzantine tombs blanket the steep necropolis on the south side of the ravine.

A fine temple doorway, thought to date from the 2nd century BC, may be seen among the jungle of vegetation at Olympus

On the north side of the stream the smooth stone doorway of a temple which housed a statue of Marcus Aurelius splits the entangled forest in two. A trail through this doorway leads to roofed Roman baths complete with mosaic floors decorated in bold geometric shapes.

There is, as yet, no modern village nearby, no tourist hotels, no distracting clamour: only an occasional farmer's cottage and a small *pension* a mile down the beach. As part of the Olympic National Forest, the area is protected from development. Two small winding roads lead down to the site from the high

THE MEDITERRANEAN COAST

coastal road; the better one comes from Kumluca, through Cavuskoy. The most spectacular approach, however, is by sea from the west. Less than ¼ mile away a wall of mountain blocks the view to the west and a two mile expanse of beach, backed by lofty Mount Olympus, is visible on the right, but the ruins of Olympus itself are neatly hidden from sight. Not until a final small headland is rounded can the seafarer look to the west and see a narrow gorge carved through the mountains.

Crumbling walls and towers are just visible above the tree tops on both slopes.

In its golden age the port must have been full of ships, the streets full of people, and the steep hillsides full of stately buildings.

End of excursions

MERSIN

With its shady, palm-lined avenues, city park and modern hotels, and surrounded by lush market gardens, Mersin is an attractive and convenient base from which to visit nearby historical sites and the numerous beaches and coves in the vicinity, all ripe for discovery. The largest port on the Turkish Mediterranean, with a regular car ferry service to Cyprus, Mersin is a rapidly developing city, with an attractive waterfront decked with gardens and trees. The old part of town contains numerous shops and reasonably-priced restaurants.

Tourism bureau: Inonu Bulv. Liman Giris Unitesi (tel: (741) 11265, 12710).

Excursion

TARSUS

About half-an-hour's drive from Mersin is Tarsus, renowned as the birthplace of the Apostle St Paul. It is also the place where Cleopatra had her first meeting with Mark Antony.

End of excursion

SIDE

An ancient fishing village situated about 50 miles (80km) east of Antalya and surrounded by fertile green plains, Side is developing into one of Turkey's premier holiday resorts, with extensive tourist development in the form of hotels and holiday villages still taking place.

Side's popularity is based on the resort's beautiful beaches, fascinating classical ruins and its friendly, informal atmosphere. The colourful main thoroughfare, now filled with an array of craft shops, bars and restaurants, follows the route of the original Roman colonnaded street. At one end are the well-preserved amphitheatre and the old Roman baths, which now house the impressive Side Museum.

The exact date of Side's foundation is not clear, although it is thought it was established in the 7th century BC as a colony of the Aeolian city of Cyme. The city really began to flourish in the 2nd century BC, when most of its income derived from the slave trade, it being the principal port in the region for the landing of slaves taken by the corsairs. The pirates were finally crushed in 67BC, so ending Side's prosperity.

Cleopatra is supposed to have bathed in the sea at Side, after an assignation with Mark Antony

It flourished again in the 2nd century AD, when much of its income was used to adorn the city with magnificent buildings; it is the remains of these which have survived. As Rome's power declined, so too did Side's importance, though it flourished once again in early Byzantine times, only to decline finally with the Arab invasions that started in the middle of the 7th century, and it was eventually destroyed by fire in the 10th century. For the next thousand years it was left deserted.

Roman Agora

Among the many ruins are those of the immense Roman agora, built in the 2nd century BC and consisting of the usual porticoed court lined with vaulted shops. The ruins of a round structure at the centre of the agora are believed to be those of a Temple of Tyche, the goddess of fortune.

Roman Baths

Directly across from the agora are the Roman baths, which have been superbly restored and now house a delightful museum exhibiting some of the finest Roman statues in Asia Minor, all of them discovered on the site in recent years.

Theatre

Just beyond the agora is the Roman theatre, the most impressive monument in Side. This was built in the 2nd century AD, and is similar to that at Aspendos. In later Roman times the orchestra was used for the performance of gladiatorial combats, and in the 5th century two open-air Christian sanctuaries were constructed there, with the congregation seated in the auditorium. There is an excellent panorama from the upper tier of the theatre, with the whole of the ancient city and its surroundings, together with the sandy beaches, stretching away on either side into the distance.

Inner Walls
The theatre formed part of the inner wall of the city, built in the 4th century AD, and the main gate through this wall leads to the ruins of a late Roman temple of Dionysus. From there the road goes straight out towards the end of the peninsula, following the course of an ancient colonnaded street.

Harbour
At the south side of the ancient harbour, now almost completely sanded up, are the remains of two adjoining temples, one dedicated to Athena and the other to Apollo. Behind these is a Byzantine basilica, and nearby is a temple dedicated to Man, the Anatolian God of the Moon.

Sports
Side offers good watersports facilities including windsurfing, waterskiing and sailing, as well as swimming and snorkelling. Many hotels also have tennis and table tennis facilities.

Hotels
The **Defne Hotel**, on the far side of the beach, has a comprehensive range of facilities, as does the **Turtel**. **Tourism bureau:** Side Yolu Uzeri (tel. (3213) 0303/265). Located at the entrance crossroads into Side.

Excursions from Side
Side's historical ruins are among the best in the area and provide a fascinating insight into Turkey's past. There are also several

other well-preserved sites worth exploring in the vicinity, at Perge, Aspendos and Termessos. Alternatively, you can take a day off to relax with a leisurely cruise on the Manavgat River to the waterfalls, and watch kingfishers and terrapins diving among the reeds, or visit Alanya or Antalya with their good shopping facilities.

HOW TO GET TO THE MEDITERRANEAN COAST

By Air
Regular scheduled and charter flights operate from many international airports to Antalya, although these tend to be less frequent in the winter. It is also possible to fly to Istanbul or Ankara and take a connecting scheduled flight to Antalya. Coach and taxi services are available from Antalya Airport to the centre of town.
Approximate distances by road from Antalya to the principal Turkish Mediterranean holiday resorts are: Kemer 21¾ miles (35km), Side 43½ miles (70km), Alanya 84 miles (135km).
Some of the Mediterranean resorts are more easily accessible from Dalaman Airport, such as Kas, which is 98 miles (158km) from Dalaman, but 123 miles (198km) from Antalya.

By Boat
Frequent services and cruises are operated to the principal ports on the Mediterranean coast by a number of lines. Also, Turkish Maritime Lines operates summer services from Istanbul and Izmir, stopping at Fethiye, Kas, Finike, Antalya, Alanya and Mersin.

CENTRAL TURKEY

Central Turkey is home to one of the country's most impressive natural wonders: the amazing region of ancient Cappadocia, with its awe-inspiring rock cones, canyons, churches, capped pinnacles and underground cities. Visits to Cappadocia are extensively featured by tour companies, either as an integral part of a coach tour of the country, or as organised excursions from the premier Aegean and Mediterranean holiday resorts, and the region is also attracting increasing numbers of visitors on fly/drive packages.

Ankara, Turkey's capital, is also located in the country's heartland, which is officially known as Central Anatolia, as is the city of Konya, one of Turkey's oldest continuously inhabited sites and home of the Mevlevi sect, internationally known as the Whirling Dervishes. Slashed by ravines and dotted with volcanic peaks, the Central Anatolian plateau—one of the cradles of civilisation—is covered with wheat fields and lines of poplars in the valleys. In its turbulent history the region has seen the march of such invaders as Alexander the Great and Tamerlane, and everywhere is evidence of the various influences that have been at work, from the Christian frescos in the rock churches of Cappadocia's Goreme valley, to Seljuk architecture in Konya.

The remarkable lunar landscape of the Goreme valley, Cappadocia, was formed through volcanic activity

◆◆◆
ANKARA

On a hill overlooking the Turkish capital of Ankara is an imposing monument to the man without whom this land of dramatic physical contrasts would have been reduced to little more than a patch of steppeland: General Mustafa Kemal. It was he who roused a people already exhausted by the Ottoman defeat in World War I, drove the invading forces into the sea, and won back for the Turks their homeland. Given the name Ataturk ('Father of the Turks'), Mustafa Kemal founded the Turkish Republic in 1923 and became its first president. Anxious to distance himself and his Republic from the Ottoman years, he decided to shift the capital from Istanbul and create a brand new one on the Anatolian plains, basing it on what was then a small town with a population of about 75,000. Today, Ankara has a population of over three million, and is growing fast.

Though the city is thoroughly modern in appearance, there were settlements on this spot as far back as 1500BC, the town's fortunes being governed by its position near the centre of the vast Anatolian plateau, making it a prosperous stopping-off point on major trade routes. In the 8th century BC the Phrygians established the city of Ancyra on the site, and five centuries later the Galatians made Ancyra their capital.

Modern Ankara has few remaining vestiges of its past, and in most respects is much less interesting to the visitor than Istanbul. Nevertheless, interspersed among the many modern office buildings and shops is evidence of its not-forgotten past: an ancient citadel, Roman baths and Ottoman mosques.

One aspect of Ankara that takes many visitors by surprise, and pleasantly so, is the city's greenery. Ataturk loved trees and had them planted practically everywhere, surrounding the city with a delightful green belt in spite of the area's instrinsically harsh terrain. And on the outskirts he built a model farm where, today, Ankara residents and visitors go to enjoy the scenery and the fresh air.

Citadel

Ankara's citadel dominates the top of a rocky summit. Its inner section was built in the 7th century when Arab invasions were particularly frequent in Asia Minor. In the 9th century Mihail II had a second wall built round the first to help fortify the citadel against invasion. This outer wall surrounds the fortress in the shape of a heart.

In its long history the citadel has been captured and damaged a number of times, yet 15 towers are still standing. Although the actual form of these walls dates from Byzantine and Seljuk times, the building material, such as marble, came from the Romans. Within the castle is a warren of narrow lanes flanked by numerous 17th- and 18th-century wooden houses, where life goes on much as it has for centuries.

Temple of Augustus

This was originally built in the 2nd century BC, and was first

Ankara is the embodiment of 20th-century Turkey, but the occasional maze of narrow cobbled streets survives

dedicated to Cybele, the mother goddess of the Anatolians, then to the Phrygian god of the moon; and finally to the Emperor Augustus. In the 4th century AD, after various alterations, it was converted into a Byzantine church.

Roman Baths

Located to the west of the Temple of Augustus, these 3rd-century baths were built by the Emperor Caracalla and dedicated to Asclepius, god of health. They were destroyed by fire in the 10th century, but remain fine examples of Roman architecture, notable for their column-adorned passage, vast dimensions and the impressive pathway to the gymnasium.

Museum of Anatolian Civilisations

Housed in two 15th-century buildings skilfully combined to form a whole, the museum is one of the most impressive in Turkey: a treasure-house of archaeological finds, including the biggest and finest collection of Hittite art and craft in the world. Beautiful pottery, finely-worked gold jewellery and miniature statuary are among the most impressive exhibits.

Ataturk Mausoleum

Begun in 1944 and completed in 1953, this mausoleum to the man who, more than anyone else, brought Turkey into the 20th century, stands 21m (60ft) high and was built in the classical style. It has a porch with a monumental staircase (33 steps in all) decorated with bas reliefs. The Tower of Liberty stands to the right of this staircase; the Tower of Independence to the left. Before the stairway is an imposing paved esplanade lined with galleries and museums, its towers symbolising the Republic, the Revolution, Victory and Peace. A magnificent processional avenue, flanked by cypress trees and 12 Hittite lions, comes to an end at the esplanade.

The mausoleum proper contains a huge inscription on its outside walls: part of a speech given by Ataturk and known as 'The Testament to Youth'. The mausoleum was designed in the form of a temple, surrounded by porticos with quadrangular pillars of fine limestone. The walls of the main funerary chamber are faced with white, red-veined marble, and the ceiling is sumptuously decorated with golden mosaics of purely Turkish motifs. The bronze doors were made in Italy and the tomb itself is a single block of marble weighing 40 tons.

Column of Julian

The Column of Julian, which stands 17m high, is thought to have been erected towards the end of the 4th century to commemorate the visit of the Emperor Julian to the city. Composed of fluted stones, it has a capital decorated with acanthus ornaments.

Haci Bayram Mosque

Built in the first half of the 15th century, this mosque was decorated by the well-known artist Mustafa towards the end of the 17th century and ornamented with Kutahya tiles in the early 18th century. The

Tomb of Haci Bayram Veli, after whom the mosque was named, is adjacent.

Hotels and Restaurants

There is a good range of hotels in all price brackets. Recommended establishments at the upper end of the scale include the 5-star **Buyuk Ankara**, on Ataturk Bulvari, and **Etap Altinel**, on Gazi Mustafa Kemal Bulvari.

Among the many excellent restaurants, the **Liman**, which specialises in fish, and the more expensive **R.V.**, in the Embassy quarter, are particularly recommended.

Tourism bureau: G.M.K. Bulv. 33 (tel: (4) 2301911, 2301915, 3217380). Central office: Istanbul Cad. 4 Ulus (tel: 3112247, 3123525, 3104960).

CAPPADOCIA

The story of Cappadocia begins about one million years ago, when the volcanoes of Erciyes and Hasadag erupted time after time, covering the Central Anatolian plateau with a thick layer of lava and volcanic ash. As the violent underground upheavals diminished, it was the turn of rain, snow, wind and extremes of temperature to do their part in eroding and sculpting the volcanic rock into the surrealist landscape we see today. The shape of the hard basalt far beneath also played its part, by resising the erosion to which the malleable volcanic rock submitted so willingly. Described by the Turkish tourism authorities as 'fairy chimneys', the rocky outcrops in Cappadocia's Zelve valley in

In Cappadocia life continues much as it has always done; tourism is an unknown new ingredient

particular vary in colour like stone chameleons, from ash grey to beige, yellow, rust and brick red, depending on the time of day. Not to be missed if at all possible is the view of this valley at sunset. As the last light of the sun slips away, combinations of navy blue, lilac, green, pale pink and gold highlights change constantly until they make way for the mysterious silvery shadows of the moonlit landscape.

Cappadocia abounds in myths and legends about giants, fairies and genies, originating in the days when men had no explanation for this extraordinary landscape. Indeed, it needs no unusual imagination to see the terrain peopled with dervishes, giants and other figures turned to stone: the guardians of a natural wonderland.

History

From the third millennium BC there were small city states in the area, and during the Hattian, Proto-Hattian and Hittite periods the region gained strategic importance due to its position on the trade route to Persia. With the fall of the Hittite Empire in the 12th century BC, the Anatolian dark ages began. Little is known about this period, but the dark ages can be said to have ended when the Lydians gained domination of Anatolia at the beginning of the 6th century BC. In 334BC Anatolia was conquered by Alexander the Great, and until AD17, when the region became a province of the Roman Empire, life went its relatively peaceful way under the rule of local dynasties. Neither the Romans nor the Byzantines made any effort to assimilate Anatolia into their own cultures. They were concerned with it only for its strategic trade location, and as a source of manpower for their armies. From the east, across Anatolia, came cotton, lemons, melons, sesame, figs, ducks and other commodities. While the Romans founded cities along this trade route through Central Anatolia, the local people preferred the rocky valleys of Cappadocia, usually hollowing their houses out of the soft rock. For heat insulation, these rock homes match up to the best modern technology, and still today the local inhabitants are waging a struggle to be allowed to go on living in their traditional homes. Throughout the ages Cappadocia has been not only a trade crossroads but also a cultural melting pot where different philosophies, cultures and religions mingled and interacted. When St Paul passed through Cappadocia in the first century he observed that the people worshipped such diverse gods as Zeus, Mitra, Attis and Dionysus, and the new doctrines of Christianity had to put forward convincing arguments against all these different pagan beliefs in order to supplant them. Yet it was here that the early Christians, fleeing first from Roman and later from Arab persecution, took refuge and built their churches, monasteries and underground cities in the rock.

The tiny picturesque churches hollowed out of the cliffs were painted and adorned with frescos, in which recurring figures include Anastasius, Gregory, John Chrisostomus and Basil of Caesarea. Basil stands out from the others for his extensive culture, tolerance, knowledge and enlightened teaching, and was known by his contemporaries as the 'Pillar of Truth' and 'Interpreter of the Heavens'.

By the time the Seljuk Turks entered Cappadocia in the second half of the 11th century, over one thousand sects existed there. Such amicable relations were established between the Christians of Cappadocia and the Seljuks that pictures of Seljuk sultans shared the walls with Orthodox saints. Like the Roman

In the village of Urgup, with its enormous cliff of volcanic rock, houses are often built adjoining the rock pyramids

and Byzantine conquerors before them, the Seljuks were more concerned with their economies than anything else, and all along the trade route known as the Sultan's Road passing through Konya, Kayseri and Sivas, they built caravanserais and mosques, many of which are still standing today.

In the mid-13th century the Moghul invasions brought the Seljuk Empire tumbling, and Anatolia was divided into a number of principalities, of which Karamanoglu, the most powerful, ruled until the Ottoman Empire won control of the region in the 14th century. Under the Turkish-Greek Population

Exchange Agreement of the 1920s, nearly all the Greek Orthodox community of Cappadocia migrated to Greece.

What to see in Cappadocia

Aksaray

A journey east across the vast Konya plain takes us to the beautiful Sultan Khan (caravanserai), 30 miles (48km) west of Aksaray. Built in 1229 during the reign of the Seljuk Sultan Keykubat I, this magnificent building features the carved stone portal so characteristic of Seljuk architecture, watchtowers, high plain walls for defence, a small mosque in the courtyard, a kitchen, bedrooms, workshops, baths and stables.

Out on the monotonous steppe landscape, Aksaray—with its poplars, pines, willows and fruit orchards—emerges into view like an oasis. An important halt on the trade route throughout history, Aksaray was founded by the Hittites, but its remaining monuments all date from the Seljuk and Karamanoglu periods.

Ihlara

Seven miles (12km) from Aksaray, a side road branches off to the right, through typical Cappadocian villages that give one the impression of being cut off completely from the outside world, to the valley of Ihlara. Through this sheer-sided valley, 6 miles (10km) long, flows the Melendis Stream, which carries the perpetually melting snows of Hasandagi and is bordered by poplars, cypresses and pistachio trees. A total of 435 steps follow a steep winding path into the valley, in whose depths are around 100 rock churches and innumerable rock houses.

Underground Cities

The Nigde road south of Nevsehir takes you to two of the underground cities in the area: Kaymakli and Derinkuyu. Although used subsequently by Christians fleeing persecution, they are pre-Christian in origin, and consist of a labyrinth of underground tunnels and chambers forming numerous storeys. The upper storeys were used as a church and living quarters, while the lower storeys consisted of storage rooms. The labyrinths were designed in such a way that even if the main entrance were discovered it would be impossible to find the way to the shelters. Moreover, upright grinding stones were placed ready to block the entrances at a moment's notice. Descending to a total depth of 40m, the underground cities were linked to one another by tunnels, and also supplied with a steady stream of fresh air via efficient ventilation systems. Guides with a reasonably good command of several languages are usually readily available to show you round.

Goreme Valley

Lying 11 miles (18km) northwest of Urgup, the Goreme Valley contains numerous rock churches boasting wonderful frescos. Most of the chapels date

A rock house in Goreme, complete with precarious outside ladder linking the different levels

from the 10th and 11th centuries of the Byzantine period. Among the most visited of these churches are the Elmali Kilise (Church with an Apple), the smallest and most recent of the group; the Karanlik Kilise (Dark Church), with its fine paintings and table and benches carved from the rock; the Carikli Kilise (Church with Sandals), so called because of the two footprints under the fresco of the Ascension; and the Yilanli Kilise (Church with Snakes), which has fascinating frescos of the damned in the coils of serpents. A short way from the main Goreme group, on the road to Avcilar, is the Tokali Kilise (Church with a Buckle), decorated with very fine 10th-century New Testament scenes. Scattered around the valley are many interesting but less accessible churches, while on the road leading north are the troglodyte village of Avcilar, with its houses attached to rock cones; Cavusin, with its churches in a rock face; the red-coned monastic complex of Zelve; and, finally, Avanos, a village famous for its pottery and onyx.

Urgup

About 6 miles (10km) from Goreme is Urgup, the oldest settlement in the area, set against an enormous cliff of volcanic rock, where the pinnacles of rock, as impressive as they are plain, are the most popular scene on postcards.

Hotels

Most of the hotels serving visitors to Cappadocia are in either Nevsehir or Urgup. Among those recommended in the former are

The interior of the Alaeddin Mosque in Konya, which was built in 1221; the columns that support the ceiling were taken from an ancient Graeco-Roman site

the **Orsan Kapadokya Hotel**, and in the latter the **Turban Holiday Village** and the **Buyuk Hotel**.

Tourism bureau: Kayseri Cad 37, Urgup (tel: (4868) 1059).

KONYA

The city of Konya, which lies at the heart of the Anatolian plateau 160 miles (260km) south of Ankara, is attracting ever-increasing numbers of international visitors for two main reasons: its beautiful Seljuk architecture, and the Mausoleum of the poet, scholar, mystic and philosopher Mevlana Celaleddin Rumi (1207–73), founder of the sect known throughout the world as the Whirling Dervishes.
Konya is an ancient city; indeed, according to Phrygian legend, it was the first city to emerge after the Flood. There was a

prehistoric and, later, a Hittite settlement here, but the first important town was founded by the Phrygians, who were succeeded by the Lydians, Persians and the Seleucid kings of Pergamon.
It was in the 12th century that the Konya Plain experienced its second cultural renaissance when the city became the capital of the Seljuk Turks. Migrating from the steppes of Central Asia, the Seljuks served the Byzantines a crushing defeat in 1071 at Malazgirt, which opened the floodgates to the Turkish settlement of Anatolia. Under the enlightened rule of the Sultan Alaeddin Keykubat, Seljuk culture reached its zenith in 13th-century Konya. It was in this environment that one of the great Moslem mystic movements was born.
Mevlana's doctrine was the seeking after good in all its positive manifestations, together with the practice of infinite tolerance. He condemned slavery and advocated

CENTRAL TURKEY

monogamy; and recognised that man must earn his bread by the sweat of his brow. As the symbol of the shedding of earthly ties, he devised the whirling dance, accompanied by the ethereal sound of the reed flute. This whirling dance can still be seen each December, during the annual Mevlana Festival.

Mevlana Mausoleum
The most famous building in Konya, not surprisingly, is the Mevlana Mausoleum, in the old monastery where the Order of Dervishes was founded. It is also the city's best known landmark. Dominated by a conical, turquoise-blue dome, the complex now houses a remarkable museum of Islamic art, as well as Rumi's sarcophagus. Of special interest are the earliest manuscript of Mevlana's great mystic epic poem, *The Mesnevi*, and some of the few surviving illuminated manuscripts, as well as early musical instruments, Dervish garments, carpets, silks, fine prayer rugs, and a mass of finely crafted religious artefacts.

Alaeddin Mosque
Completed during the reign of Alaeddin Keykubat, this mosque is in the Syrian style, unusual for Anatolia, with a wooden ceiling instead of a high dome, and simple, unadorned brick arches supported by 42 columns. The pulpit and altar are masterpieces of wood-carving.

Karatay Medresesi
Now housing the Museum of Ceramic Art, containing lovely displays of rare Seljuk ceramics, this was built in the 13th century. The interior of the building,

formerly a theological college, is itself a riot of beautiful blue tiles.

Hotels
Of the numerous hotels and *pensions* in Konya, the **Ozkaymak Park** and the **Selcuk** are two of the best.
Tourism bureau: Mevlana Cad. 21 (tel: (331) 11074). Near the Mevlana Museum.

HOW TO GET TO CENTRAL TURKEY

By Air
Ankara Airport is well served by scheduled flights from major international cities. In addition, numerous domestic flights connect Ankara with Turkey's regional airports. The airport at Konya is also served by domestic flights.

By Road
Ankara is also well served by bus services, approximate road distances being Istanbul 272 miles (438km), Izmir 370 miles (595km), Konya 163 miles (262km), Cappadocia 174 miles (280km). The three-lane E5 road from Istanbul is the busiest highway in Turkey, and traffic delays are frequent.

By Rail
Between Istanbul and Ankara there are frequent day and night express services, and between Ankara and Keyseri there is also a regular express service. Car-trains operate from Istanbul to Konya. The Istanbul–Ankara Blue Train (Mavi Tren) takes about 7½ hours, while the alternative is the Anatolia Express night train, with sleeping cars. From Izmir there are regular express trains to Ankara, taking about 11 hours.

ISTANBUL

Istanbul is one of the world's most fascinating and exciting cities. Its intriguing blend of old and new, East and West, combined with its strategic setting bridging the continents of Europe and Asia, make a visit here unforgettable. As former capital of three world empires, Istanbul's contrasts are apparent everywhere, from the sirens of the ships to the timeless sounds of 'muezzins' calling the faithful to prayer; from the sunlight flashing off the golden crescent of the mosque domes to the hypnotic gaze of Byzantine mosaic figures. But Istanbul is not just historic— it is still a great city, vividly alive. Beneath the little-changing skyline of its domes and minarets there is the continual bustle and movement of the crowd; the rumbling of

vehicles along ancient cobbled streets; the incessant coming and going of the ferries; and the cries of street-sellers mingling with the sounds of shipping in the busy port.

The old city is set on a triangular promontory between the Golden Horn and the Sea of Marmara, and is defended on the landward side by its massive Byzantine walls, now being painstakingly restored on the initiative of Istanbul's enterprising Mayor. Here the Emperor Justinian built Christendom's greatest church, St Sophia, now a museum. Facing St Sophia is the elegant mosque of Sultan Ahmet I, better known as the Blue Mosque because of its magnificent

There are magnificent views across the Bosphorus from the top of Topkapi Palace, Istanbul

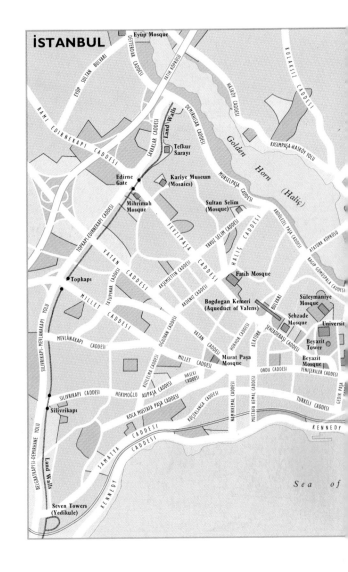

İSTANBUL

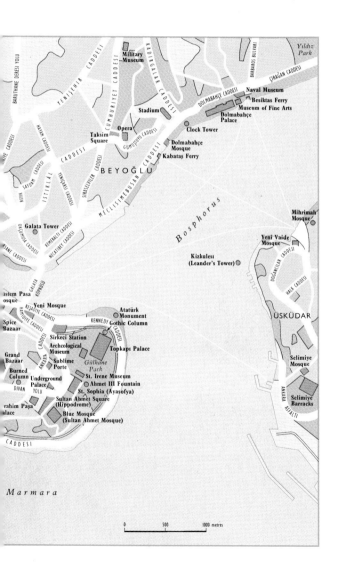

ISTANBUL AND SURROUNDINGS

internal decoration of blue Iznik tiles. Another of Istanbul's most magical tourist sights is Topkapi Palace, former residence of the Ottoman rulers and now an irresistible museum housing a wealth of treasures.

A visit to Istanbul's world-famous Grand Bazaar, with its staggering collection of 4,000 shops, is also high on most visitors' list of priorities, if only to soak up the wonderful Oriental atmosphere. Shopping, indeed, is one of the many delights of a visit to Istanbul, and as well as the unique appeal of the Grand Bazaar, the city's modern streets contain boutiques selling up-to-the-minute fashions, while just about everywhere you will encounter the more traditional shops selling items of silver, gold, leather and all manner of hand-crafted articles.

During the past few years a major programme of reconstruction and restoration work has started to beautify the city and to preserve many of its most important quarters, buildings and monuments.

In the recent past, for instance, the famous Golden Horn had become heavily polluted by industrial waste from nearby factories. Now, these factories have been demolished and the banks of the inlet turned into green parks. Meanwhile, water pipes along the banks carry sewage off to the depths of the Marmara Sea. The construction of the new Galata Bridge spanning the Golden Horn at its mouth and connecting major commercial districts on both banks is a major step in speeding up the flow of traffic in the densely populated areas of the city, while at Aksaray the first section of a long-awaited metro system has been completed. Another major undertaking is the restoration of the ancient land walls of the city, spanning the west side of the peninsula and connecting the sea walls along the Golden Horn in the north and those along the Sea of Marmara in the south. After the restoration, many of the moats outside the walls will be filled with water, and other plans call for the building of open air theatres, parks and sports facilities.

The Turkish Touring and Automobile Association has also been playing a major role in Istanbul's beautification, having restored and converted two old mansions into stylish hotels, and restored and opened up to the public numerous attractive tea houses and restaurants in the city's many parks.

These, and many other improvement schemes taking place throughout Istanbul, are adding considerably to the city's attractions, making a visit here of even a week too short a time to soak up its atmosphere and savour its splendours: the ancient churches, mosques, palaces, bazaars and restaurants, coffee shops and tea houses, delightful parks, and exotic nightlife, not to mention fascinating excursions along the Bosphorus, with perhaps a delicious freshly-caught seafood lunch on one of the surrounding islands.

Istanbul has an exotic style all of its own, which cannot compare with any other capital or city in Europe.

The Harem in Topkapi, popular with tourists, conjures up many a colourful tale

What to see in Istanbul

Palaces

◆◆◆
TOPKAPI PALACE
No visit to Istanbul would be complete without a trip to the amazing Topkapi Palace, former residence of the Ottoman rulers and now a museum housing a wealth of treasures, including a priceless collection of exquisite Chinese porcelain, a display of famous jewels from the Imperial Treasury, and an exhibition of the robes worn by the sultans and their families.

The jewels of the Treasury are particularly impressive: an Aladdin's cave overspilling into four rooms. The breathtaking effect is enhanced by the display of turban crests, jewel-studded armour and helmets, every possible utensil and weapon encrusted with diamonds and pearls, and no fewer than three thrones. The famous emerald dagger, star of the film *Topkapi*, is outshone by the 84-carat Spoonmaker diamond.

Beside the imposing gate to the palace is the elegant fountain of Sultan Ahmet III. In the first court stands the ancient Church of St Irene, one of the oldest Christian churches in Istanbul, and on the left of the second court, shaded by cypresses and plane trees, is the palace kitchen, now housing an exquisite collection of Chinese porcelain.

The harem, entered through a gate on the right side of the court, was the secluded quarters of the wives and concubines of the sultan. In the third court is the Hall of Audience of the sultan, then the library of Ahmet III. This leads to an exhibition of robes worn by the sultans and their families, the jewel display, and finally an exhibition of miniatures. In the fourth court is the Pavilion of the Holy Mantle, enshrining relics of the Prophet Mohammed.

◆◆◆
DOLMABAHCE PALACE

Built in the mid-19th century by Sultan Abdulmecit, the palace is imposingly located, with a huge frontage on to the Bosphorus. Particularly impressive is the vast reception salon supported by 56 columns, containing a huge crystal chandelier. Also of special interest are the harem and the Bird Pavilion, where birds from all over the world were kept.

◆◆
BEYLERBEYI PALACE

Located on the Asian side of the Bosphorus, this palace was built by Sultan Abdulaziz in 1865 of white marble, and possesses a beautiful garden adorned with magnolia trees. It was used as a summer residence of the sultans and a guesthouse for visiting foreign dignitaries.

◆◆
YILDIZ PALACE

This is a complex of pavilions, a palace and a mosque built over a long period of time and by several sultans but completed by Abdulhamit II at the end of the 19th century. The Sale, largest and most splendid of the buildings, reflects the luxurious lifestyle of the period. The palace is set in a very large garden of flowers, plants and trees brought from every part of the world and, being situated on the crest of a hill, offers panoramic views of Istanbul and the river.

Museums

◆◆◆
ST SOPHIA (AYASOFYA)

The present St Sophia is the third building with this name to occupy the same site. The first church was completed in 366 in the reign of Constantius, son of Constantine the Great. This church was destroyed by fire in 404, and a new church was later built on the same site by Theodosius II, and dedicated in 415, but this, too, was destroyed by fire in 532. Emperor Justinian began work on the present basilica in 532 and it was completed in 537. Designed by Anthemius and the architect Isidorus, the building immediately earned far-reaching admiration both for its

Originally modelled on the Church of the Holy Sepulchre, St Sophia became a mosque in the 16th century

dome and for its dazzling ornamentation.

The basilica underwent repairs in 994. Later it was looted by European Christians who came to Istanbul with the army of the Fourth Crusade. According to accounts of Russian priests who visited Istanbul in the 15th century, St Sophia was in a virtually abandoned state at that period. In 1453, with the conquest of Istanbul by the Turks, the building was taken over and reorganised. Remains from such ancient cities as Sheba, Ephesus and Baalbek were used in the building's reconstruction and the original walls of St Sophia were decorated with coloured marble and mosaics.

Inside, above the south door of the building—used these days as the main entrance—is a striking mosaic depicting Mary sitting on a throne, with the Infant Jesus on her lap and two figures to her left and right. The figure on the left is Constantine the Great, presenting to Mary the city which he founded; and on the right is St Justinian, offering a model of St Sophia.

Above the building's actual main door, the Emperor's Gate, is a mosaic portraying Jesus, Mary and the Angel Gabriel. Jesus holds in his left hand a book upon which is written 'I am the Peace of the World and the Light'. Rampways on four sides of the building lead to the upper galleries. The western side of the top-floor galleries was reserved for the Empress and for the wives of the leading members of the state. In the south gallery there is a section known as the Consul's Meeting Hall.

In the middle of the right-hand wall of the hall is a mosaic portraying Jesus, Mary and John the Baptist, while on the east wall are depicted the Emperor Constantine and the Empress Zoe offering to an enthroned Jesus a purse of gold and the imperial edict which ordered the creation of the city.

A delightful café, the Ayasofya, is located in a quiet corner of the museum's garden in the shade of ancient trees.

◆◆
KARIYE MUSEUM

The 11th-century St Saviour in Chora is, after St Sophia, the most important Byzantine monument in Istanbul. The walls are decorated with superb 14th-century frescos and mosaics on a gold background. The church is a remarkable museum of Byzantine art, and has a quiet, carefully tended garden facing old wooden houses where you can sip your tea or coffee restfully.

ST IRENE MUSEUM
St Irene was the first church in Istanbul and was built by Constantine in the 4th century and rebuilt by Justinian. It is reputedly the site of a pre-Christian temple.

ARCHAEOLOGICAL MUSEUMS
These are situated at the boundary of the first court of the Topkapi Palace. The rich collection of antiquities in the Archaeological Museum includes the celebrated Alexander Sarcophagus, while the Museum of the Ancient Orient displays antiquities from the Hatti, Hittite, Assyrian, Babylonian and Sumerian civilisations.

CINILI KOSK (Museum of Turkish Ceramics)
This pavilion was built by Sultan Mehmet in the 15th century and contains beautiful Iznik tiles from the 16th century and fine Seljuk and Ottoman examples.

IBRAHIM PASA PALACE (Museum of Turkish and Islamic Art)
Built in 1524 by Ibrahim Pasa, Grand Vizier of Suleyman the Magnificent, the palace was the grandest private residence ever constructed in the Ottoman empire. It is now a museum containing many beautiful Turkish and Persian miniatures, Seljuk tiles and antique carpets.

NAVAL MUSEUM
Located in the Besiktas neighbourhood, this museum contains the great imperial caiques that were used to row the sultans across the Bosphorus, as well as many interesting exhibits from Ottoman naval history.

MILITARY MUSEUM
The exhibits from Ottoman history on show here include the great field tents used on campaigns.

ATATURK MUSEUM
The house where Ataturk lived in Sisli contains his personal effects.

SADBERK HANIM MUSEUM
A charming museum dedicated to old Turkish arts and handicrafts, situated on the Bosphorus at Buyukdere.

MUSEUM OF FINE ARTS
Located at Besiktas, this is widely considered one of the finest museums in Turkey, housing paintings and sculptures from the end of the 19th century to the present day.

MUSEUM OF TURKISH CARPETS
Near the Sultan Ahmet Mosque, it contains a fine collection of Turkish carpets and *kilims*, including some of the oldest examples in existence.

Mosques

◆◆◆
THE BLUE MOSQUE (Sultan Ahmet Camii)

Facing St Sophia is the elegant mosque of Sultan Ahmet I, known as the Blue Mosque because of its magnificent interior of turquoise-blue Iznik tiles. It is the only mosque to have six minarets.

◆◆
SULEYMANIYE MOSQUE

The mosque of Suleyman the Magnificent is considered the most beautiful and splendid of all the imperial mosques in Istanbul. It was built between 1550 and 1557 by the famous architect Sinan, whose goal was to surpass the builders of St Sophia. Standing on a hill, it is conspicuous by its great size, emphasised by the four minarets rising one from each corner of the courtyard. Inside, the *mihrab* (prayer-niche) and *mimber* (pulpit) are of finely-carved white marble, and there are fine stained glass windows. Adjoining the mosque were theological schools, a school of medicine, a soup kitchen and hospice for the poor, caravanserai, and Turkish baths.

◆
FATIH MOSQUE

This imperial mosque, constructed between 1463 and 1470, bears the name of the conqueror of Istanbul. Standing on top of one of the hills of Istanbul, it is notable for its vast size and the great complex of religious foundations surrounding it: theological schools, hospices, a hospital, caravanserai and a library.

Light pours through 260 windows in the Blue Mosque, second largest in the Moslem world, to highlight the effect of the beautiful porcelain tiles

◆
RUSTEM PASA MOSQUE

Built in 1561, the mosque of Rustem Pasa, beside the Golden Horn, was constructed by the architect Sinan on the orders of Rustem Pasa, Grand Vizier and son-in-law of Suleyman the Magnificent.

Monuments

◆◆
SULTAN AHMET SQUARE

In front of the Blue Mosque is the site of the ancient Hippodrome, scene of chariot races and the centre of Byzantine civic life. Of the monuments which once decorated it only three remain: the Obelisk of Theodosius, the bronze Serpentine Column and the Column of Constantine.

ISTANBUL AND SURROUNDINGS

AHMET III FOUNTAIN
Standing at the entrance to Topkapi Palace and built in 1729 as a gift to Ahmet III, this is one of the most magnificent free-standing fountains in the world. Highly ornamented and covered with a pointed roof with deep eaves, it is a fine example of fountain architecture.

RUMELI HISARI
The Rumelian Fortress built by Sultan Mehmet in 1452 prior to the conquest of Istanbul was completed in only four months. It is now used as the setting for some of the performances that are a feature of the annual Istanbul Festival.

GALATA TOWER
This huge tower built by the Genoese in 1348 is 62m high, and now houses a restaurant and nightclub offering wonderful views of the Golden Horn and the Bosphorus.

BEYAZIT TOWER
Situated in the grounds of Istanbul University, this 85m-high tower was built by Mahmut II in 1828 as a fire tower.

ISTANBUL LAND WALLS
Constructed in the 5th century by the Emperor Theodosius, the walls stretch 4 miles (7km) from the Sea of Marmara to the Golden Horn. With their many towers and bastions they were once the mightiest fortifications in Christendom.

BOGDOGAN KEMERI
(Aqueduct of Valens)
Built by the Emperor Valens in AD368, the aqueduct supplied the Byzantine and later the Ottoman palaces with water. A considerable length of the double-tier arches remains.

The Rumeli Hisari, or European Castle, is 6 miles (10km) north of the city at the narrowest point of the Bosphorus

KIZKULESI

Also known as Leander's Tower, this is on a tiny islet at the entrance to Istanbul harbour where Leander is supposed to have drowned when swimming the Bosphorus to get to Hero. Although first constructed in the 12th century, the present building dates from the 18th century.

Hotels

Istanbul has an excellent range of hotels in most price brackets, many located in the Taksim area, the busy centre of the new city. The **Etap Marmara** stands on Taksim Square, across from the Ataturk Cultural Centre. A deluxe hotel with 432 rooms, its rooftop Panorama Restaurant and Tepe Bar offer splendid panoramas of the city. Across the Taksim Gardens is the **Istanbul Sheraton**, which combines the luxury of an international hotel with an Oriental atmosphere. The 460 rooms are handsomely furnished, and the hotel offers a choice of restaurants, La Coupole serving both traditional and local food, and the Revan original Turkish food. Grandly decorated in Ottoman pink, the Revan commands magnificent views of the Bosphorus. Latest addition is the Café Vienna, popular for coffee, cakes and ice cream.

Close to the Sheraton, on Cumhuriyet Caddesi, is the 200-room **Divan**, whose friendly atmosphere makes it a favourite haunt of Istanbulis. The hotel is famous for its food, be it the delicious chocolates and pastries in the tea-room, the informal fare of the popular Divan Pub, or the international and Turkish cuisine of the stylish Divan Restaurant.

From the Divan, a walk along Cumhuriyet Caddesi—the long avenue lined with shops, bars, restaurants, travel agencies and airline offices—leads to the **Hilton International**, whose spacious gardens and grounds, totalling 13 acres, can easily accommodate the hotel's 526 rooms, plus a large convention centre. The Roof Rotisserie commands a panoramic view of the Bosphorus. Also popular are the Hilton's Green House Restaurant and Lalezar Bar. The hotel's sports facilities are excellent and play an important part in the social life of the city.

The smaller, 185-room **Macka Hotel** is situated in the fashionable residential district of Macka. It has a good restaurant, and is within easy walking distance of the better shops and restaurants in the area.

Dominating the beautiful bay of Tarabya on the Bosphorus is the **Buyuk (Grand) Tarabya**, a 20-minute drive from the city centre. Its 261 rooms face the bay. The Bogazici Restaurant and the Teras Restaurant are always crowded in the summer.

An airport hotel with a difference is the **Cinar Hotel** in Yesilkoy. Just 2½ miles (4km) from the airport and 10 miles (16km) from the city, the Cinar has a huge swimming pool and private beach. Its two restaurants are the Mehtap Grill, for Turkish specialities, or the Perigourdine, for dinner and dancing as well as a live show.

For those who prefer the quiet elegance of an Ottoman villa in the heart of the historic city, the **Yesil Ev** (formerly Yesil Konak), a beautifully-restored 19th-century mansion, is the place to stay. The high-ceilinged rooms (only 20) are comfortable and furnished with antiques. A sense of history pervades this small hotel, which is within walking distance of the Topkapi Palace, the Blue Mosque and St Sophia. On my last visit to Istanbul I enjoyed a delicious lunch in the hotel's charming and tranquil courtyard garden. Two other very stylish hotels converted from interesting old buildings are the **Ayasofia Ottoman Mansions** and the **Sokhollu Pasha**. The former is, in fact, nine hotels in one: an entire street of old wooden Ottoman houses rescued from destruction and beautifully restored to their past glory. Close to Topkapi Palace and facing St Sophia, the delightful guestrooms, each with its own individual character, are furnished in the gracious style and comfort enjoyed in Ottoman times by rich Turkish families. In addition to their antique furnishings and oriental rugs, all the rooms have modern bathrooms. In front of the row of pastel-painted houses runs a steep cobbled street, banned to traffic. The **Sokhollu Pasha**, also situated near Topkapi Palace, was built as a mansion for the eminent Sokhollu Pasha, the Ottoman Grand Vizier. Its elegant 18th-century lines have remained unchanged, and inside you will find carved Oriental furniture resting on rich Turkish carpets, a genuine Byzantine

wine cellar below ground, and an original Turkish bath available for the use of hotel guests. Outside, a gilded staircase sweeps down to the delightful gardens, with a marble fountain. Yet another interesting old building converted into an hotel is **Hidiv Kasri**, once the summer palace of the Egyptian Khedive. Overlooking the Bosphorus, this art deco palace, set in a large park, is for those seeking the opulent Istanbul of the past. The old stables have been converted into a restaurant.

One of Istanbul's oldest hotels, the **Pera Palas**, in the Tepebasi district, overlooking the Golden Horn, was built in 1892 to accommodate passengers on the Oriental Express. It is still evocative of a colourful past, while the newly-opened 275-room **Ramada Hotel**, in the old city district, offers all the modern comforts and facilities associated with international chain hotels.

Restaurants
Most of the many restaurants to be found in and around the old city are traditional and typically Turkish, such as the **Konyali Palace Restaurant** in Topkapi Palace, whose menu offers excellent, basic Turkish dishes, and delicious savoury pastries and desserts.

The **Gar (station) Restaurant** at Sirkeci Train Station has remained unchanged since 1876, when it proudly greeted passengers off the legendary Orient Express. Under an impressive, lofty ceiling, both Turkish and international cuisine of a high standard is served. The same management operates the

Istanbul is a fine place for shopping, be it street trader, bazaar or high-class international shop

Borsa Lokantasi, in the old city, which offers a typical Turkish lunch. For over 60 years it has served simple, freshly prepared Turkish specialities to the business community, and is traditional to the point of not serving alcohol; or, at least, it didn't on my last visit.

The huge dining room at the **Liman (port) Restaurant**, built in 1940, seems so close to the cruise ships lined up on the quay that you have the impression of being able to reach out and touch them. Until the 1950s the Liman catered for the grand receptions held at the Beylerbeyi and Dolmabahce Palaces and still has a faithful lunchtime clientele.

Beyti, at Florya, towards the airport, stands beside the Sea of Marmara. Despite its size—11 dining halls with ceramic tiled walls, 3 terraces and 5 kitchens—this is a culinary institution in Istanbul and one of the best places for Turkish meat dishes. For a typically Oriental flavour, **Pandelli's**, situated above the entrance to the Spice Bazaar, has small, arched rooms decorated with blue tiles. For a magnificent view of the old city, the **Galata Tower's** restaurant at the top of the 1216 Genoese tower is the place to choose. There is also a Turkish nightclub up there.

The atmosphere in the restaurants located in the modern city is more cosmopolitan and less traditional, and the clientele tends to belong to Istanbul's fashionable, international set. **The Plaza** complex, for instance, at Bronx Sokak, is close to the Macka Hotel, is the place where people gather to be seen and to see, and includes an English-style classical bar for cocktails or after-dinner drinks, a light and airy restaurant, and, next door, a discothèque. **Club 29**, with its stylish art deco interior, comes under the same ownership and has a small restaurant downstairs, specialising in French cuisine. Dancing is upstairs. In the summer, Club 29 moves to Vanikoy 29, on the Asiatic shores of the Bosphorus. A motor-boat is provided for the crossing.

Park Samdan, in Mim Kemal Oke Caddesi, close to the park, is a smart, modern restaurant decorated with mirrors, and serves excellent Turkish specialities as well as international cuisine. Its sister restaurant, **Samdan**, in Nisbetiye Caddesi, is decorated in an art deco style, specialises in Italian food and has a discothèque upstairs.

The **Abdullah Restaurant**, on the hills of Istinye, has been operating since 1881. In the summer, the Abdullah's beautiful garden is a popular spot for eating out, often used by members of the diplomatic corps.

To dine in this watery city is a delight, and the Bosphorus is lined with fish restaurants. Although most of them are good, the **Yeni-Bebek Restaurant**, with its lovely terrace on the Bay of Bebek, is favoured by locals and visitors alike for its seafood specialities. Prices here tend to be high, and in summer it is necessary to book.

The **Ziya** restaurant and bar in Macka is well known for its mezes and is popular with locals, while **Ziya** in Ortakoy attracts a young clientele for dining and dancing by the Bosphorus. Both these are no more than a 20-minute taxi-ride from the city centre.

For the best Turkish show, with Turkish music and exotic belly dancing performances, the place to dine is the **Kervansary Nightclub**, between the Divan Hotel and the Hilton. Others offering Oriental shows are the **Maksim** nightclubs (in Taksim Square and Bebek), where large orchestras accompany the Turkish singers and belly dancers.

Shopping

Istanbul is a good place for shopping, ranging from the crowded bazaars and street markets to fashionable boutiques and shops selling designer clothes.

Grand Bazaar

Kapali Carsisi, the covered bazaar in the old city—universally known as the Grand Bazaar—is the largest Oriental souk in the world: a labyrinth of streets and alleys, each specialising in different crafts and trades. The jewellery sections gleam with Oriental pieces in gold or silver, studded with diamonds, gems and precious stones; the copper and bronze section has an amazing array of objects and souvenirs; and the carpet sellers' street provides a luxurious display of colourful wool rugs, fine Hereke silk carpets, old and new woven *kilims*, *cicims* and long-haired goat rugs. In the leather section there is a wide choice of goods, although the quality varies. In the centre of the bazaar is the antique section of the Bedesten, a treasure trove of objects, from ikons, old coins, embroideries, rings, porcelain and onyx vases to weapons, stoves and braziers. Also in the bazaar, antique shops, such as **Abdullah-L. Chalabi** and **Epoque**, have fine ikons, antique jewellery and *objets d'art*. **Berfu** specialises in beautiful handmade jewellery copied from ancient designs up to 5,000 years old. Other shops stocking a large selection of fine jewellery include **Sait Koc**, **Camic** and **Lapis**.

Spice Bazaar

The Spice Bazaar, known as

The largest covered market in the world, the Grand Bazaar is full of people whose main object in life is to sell something to a tourist

Misir Carsisi, fills the air with the aroma of herbs and spices, remedial plants, roots and powders, and is the place to go to buy honey, halva, nuts and saffron.

Virtually everywhere you go in Turkey, someone will try to sell you a carpet, and this is especially true in Istanbul. If you are looking for a reliable carpet and rug shop where you can spend some time studying what is available and on display and choosing carefully, with less of the aggressive sales techniques employed by some, go to **Gallery Istanbul**, **Lapis** or **Bazaar 54**.

For a quiet browse accompanied by the inevitable glass of tea, go to the shop called **Sofa**, where you will find excellent old prints and maps, calligraphy, old and new Kutahya ceramics, second-hand rugs, *kilims* and Persian miniatures. Shops catering for more contemporary taste and stocking fashionable designer clothes can be found in Istiklal Caddesi, Cumhuriyet Caddesi and the hilly, residential area of Macka.

Tourism Bureaux:
Central office: Mesrutiyet Cad No 56/7 Galatasaray (tel: (1) 1456593, 1456875, 1492782). Harbiye: Hilton Hotel (tel: (1) 1330592). Karakoy: Karakoy Limani Yolu Salonu (tel: (1) 1495776). Sultanahmet: Divan Yolu Cad 3 (tel: (1) 5224903). Yesilkoy: Ataturk Hava Alani (tel: (1) 5737399). Yalova: Iskele Meyd 5 (tel: (1) 2108).

Excursions from Istanbul

Istanbul is a good base for exploring numerous easily-accessible interesting cities, towns, holiday resorts and islands on the Bosphorus, in the region known as Thrace, and along the Sea of Marmara. If time is at a premium, a day's visit to the Princes Islands makes a delightful outing. Also particularly popular with visitors are excursions to the holiday resort and thermal spa of Yalova, the town of Iznik, famous for its ceramic tiles, the city of Bursa, and the frontier town of Edirne, provincial capital of European Turkey.

◆◆◆
PRINCES ISLANDS

A ferry boat trip to one of the Princes Islands, in the Sea of Marmara, is a pleasant option for the visitor to Istanbul. There are 9 islands in total, only 4 of them inhabited. Most popular with visitors are Buyukada, which means Big Island, and Heybeli. The islands were once the pleasure spots of Byzantine princes; nowadays they are popular summer retreats of the city dwellers of Istanbul. On both Buyukada and Heybeli, restaurants and cafés line the waterfront by the landing stage while, because motor cars are banned, sightseeing is by means of horse-drawn buggies. Buyukada is arguably the more attractive of these two islands, with the feel of a Mediterranean resort, but both have considerable charm. Popular excursions here from Istanbul involve a morning ferry crossing, an island buggy tour, followed

by lunch in one of the many fish-speciality restaurants, and finally time for shopping or browsing before taking a late afternoon ferry back to Istanbul.

◆◆◆
YALOVA

This resort has been attracting visitors since Roman times, thanks to the presence of hot-spring mineral waters flowing from a forested hillside 7 miles (12km) away. The main baths are in Byzantine style, while a large open-air pool is fed by waters that originate at 60°C (140°F). Yalova offers a sandy beach flanked by a pleasant tree-lined promenade, and several modern hotels, while the surrounding hills are particularly popular with walkers and hikers. A summer house built for Ataturk in 1929 is open to visitors.

◆◆◆
IZNIK

The town of Iznik is rich in historic monuments. The walls surrounding it, the castle towers and the remains of Roman gates, are all evidence of the city's past importance. The first domed mosque of Ottoman architecture, the Haci Ozbek Camii, the famous tiled Green Mosque, and the Nilufer Hatun Imareti are among the impressive Islamic monuments to be seen. First settled in prehistoric times and developed in 316BC by one of Alexander the Great's generals, Iznik became famous in church history as the meeting place of the First Ecumenical Council which laid down in AD325 the first universally agreed doctrines of Christianity. During the 14th century a porcelain industry was established and this grew rapidly, thanks to constant demand for ceramics to decorate mosques, palaces and other buildings. Among the attractions awaiting visitors to this pleasant town is a 14th-century soup kitchen and a Dervish hospice, now used as a museum featuring, not surprisingly, ceramics.

◆◆◆
EDIRNE

Edirne, founded by the Roman emperor Hadrian in AD125, is situated on a slope, surrounded by the River Tunca. It is a town of attractive cobbled streets lined with ancient wooden houses, a bustling bazaar, Museum of Islamic Art, Archaeological Museum with many fine Roman statues, and a beautifully-restored caravanserai. One of Edirne's most impressive buildings is Sinan's masterpiece, the Selimiye Mosque, its vast dome surrounded by four immensely tall and slender minarets.

Edirne is also famous for the annual tournament of greased wrestling held in late June and early July on the island of Sarayici on the River Tunca, once a hunting reserve for the sultans.

◆◆◆
BURSA

There is plenty to see, too, in Bursa, capital of the Ottoman empire in the 14th century. Among its many impressive monuments is the Green Mosque, built in 1413–21, and considered to be one of the most beautiful in Turkey. Bursa is also

renowned as one of Turkey's major health and spa resorts. Standing at the foot of Uludag Mountain, the town is a meeting place for natural, cultural and historic riches. It takes its name from Prusias I, King of Bythinia, and is embellished with many very early examples of Ottoman architecture.

A visit to this green and pleasant town—Turkey's 6th largest with a population of over a million—should take in the Archaeological Museum, displaying remains from Roman and Byzantine architecture and an interesting coin collection, and the impressive blue-tiled Muradiye Camii, located next to a pretty garden which in summer is ablaze with roses and magnolia blossoms.

The tile decorations in Bursa's Green Mosque are probably the most attractive of any in Turkey

A huge reproduction wooden horse, built according to Homer's description, stands at the entrance to Troy

Ideally, a visit to Bursa would not be complete without an ascent of Uludag, especially in springtime when the plain below the mountain is a beautiful green, and the hillsides are ablaze with blossoms and wild flowers. A cable car operates from the hillside to the east of the town, or you can take a taxi up the mountain road from Cekirge. The view from the top is magnificent.
Tourism bureau: Ataturk Caddesi 82 (tel: 12359). Near the Ulu Mosque.

◆◆◆
TROY

Troy (Truva) is evocative of the epic struggle highlighted in *The Iliad*, and was believed to be only a work of Homer's

imagination until nine levels of civilisations were unearthed in the 1870s. Heinrich Schliemann found a great deal of treasure at the second from bottom layer (c.2600BC), which he believed to be Homer's Troy. More recent experts believe that Troy 6 (1900–1300BC) or Troy 7, which was destroyed by an unknown attacker in 1200BC – consistent with the legend of the Trojan War – was the Troy of *The Iliad*. There is not much to see on the site now; there is an interesting museum.
Tourism bureau: A. Hamdi Tanpinar Cad., Saydam Is Merkezi No 21, Kat. 5 (tel: (241) 228005, 227513).

HOW TO GET TO ISTANBUL

By Air
Istanbul's Ataturk Airport is well served by international airlines from most of the world's major capitals, and there are easy connections to the city's domestic airport.

By Road
Motorists coming on the E5 from Europe—158 miles (253km) from the Bulgarian border via Edirne, 156 miles (250km) from the Greek border at the Ipsala bridge—enter the old town either through the Topkapi Gate, crossing the Golden Horn by the Ataturk bridge; or by the Edirnekapi and follow the Fevzipasa Caddesi to the intersection with Ataturk Bulvari. Visitors staying in hotels in the Taksim Square district or on the Bosphorus may prefer to take the Istanbul bypass at Ataturk Airport, which leads across the Golden Horn Bridge.

THE BLACK SEA

Turkey's Black Sea shores are not as developed touristically as her Aegean and Mediterranean coasts, but with their densely forested mountains giving way to tea terraces, hazel-nut groves and tobacco plantations, and pleasant seaside resorts, they are becoming increasingly popular with international visitors.

According to legend, these shores, cut off from the rest of Turkey by the Black Sea mountain chain, were the land of the mighty Amazons, and an Amazon queen is said to have founded Sinop, famous as the birthplace of the satirist and philosopher Diogenes.

The most developed of the many coastal resorts along the Black Sea include Kilyos and Sile, not far from Istanbul, while other towns with good beaches include Akcahoca, Inkum, Amasra and Fatsa. The region is also home to the busy port of Trabzon, set in spectacular scenery, and with a rich historical heritage. Here, there are the remains of a Byzantine fortress and many ancient buildings, including the church of St Sophia with its interesting frescos and reliefs. Not far from Trabzon is the Monastery of Sumela, set like a swallow's nest on a sheer rock face.

The southern coast of the Black Sea was for centuries one of the world's busiest maritime highways. As early as 1250BC it was the route taken by the Argonauts sailing out of the Bosphorus eastwards over the perennially dark waters of this inland sea, on their way to Colchis in search of the Golden Fleece. The coast was an avenue of escape for Xenophon the Athenian and what was left of his Ten Thousand, fighting their way back home to Greece in 401–399BC. In 1295 Marco Polo, with his career in Cathay behind him,

Blue water and blue sky on the Black Sea at Sile

THE BLACK SEA

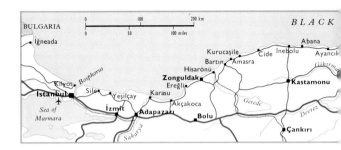

took ship at Trapezus, later Trebizond and now Trabzon, and sailed to Constantinople (now Istanbul) and at last to Italy. Kingdoms flourished and died here, like that of Mithridates the Great who defied and then succumbed to the power of Imperial Rome, and Byzantine Trabzon itself which survived Constantinople by almost a decade.

The Black Sea coast's isolation has made it strikingly different from the rest of Turkey, physically and culturally. It is cut off from the hot summers and severe winters of Anatolia by the rampart-like mountains that rise parallel to the coast. These vary in elevation from 600 to 3,000m (10,000ft) and give the coastal zone the highest rainfall of any part of Turkey, reflected by the fertility of the land.

◆
KILYOS

A snug little seaside village located some 20 miles (32km) from Istanbul and about 6 miles (10km) from the Bosphorus, Kilyos has a lovely, long wide beach of golden sand, and several hotels, restaurants, bars and shops. In the close vicinity is

some lovely scenery with many small farms scattered across the lush green fields, making this ideal walking country.

Hotels
One of the nicest hotels in the resort is the **Kilyos Kale**.

◆
SAMSUN

Samsun, called Amisus by its founders, shows no evidence of its violent past: in the first century BC its citizens burned Amisus down rather than surrender to the Romans who had laid siege to them. Fourteen centuries later the city was once again burned to the ground, this time by the Genoese traders of Amisus defending themselves from the Ottomans.

Modern Turkey was born at Samsun on 19 May 1919 when a young officer from Macedonia called Mustafa Kemal, later known as Ataturk, stepped ashore here from the steamer *Bandirma* to lead his struggling armies across Anatolia to victory at Smyrna (Izmir). He went on to form the first Turkish republic and bring the country into the 20th century, something that Samsun certainly reflects today

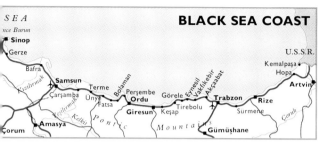

with its sprawling annual industrial and agricultural fair.

SILE

Sile has long been a popular resort with Turkish people, and is now being featured in an increasing number of foreign tour companies' brochures, thanks to its lovely beach and easy-going atmosphere. In many respects it resembles a British seaside resort: a hotch-potch of windows and balconies look down on the harbour, beaches, board-sailers, pedal-boats and bathers. Unlike Britain, however, the weather is usually reliable, with very high temperatures. There are many pleasant restaurants facing the main street, most of them offering tables with sea-views. The sea is warm and clear, and the sand perfect. The main beaches are also well equipped and, for those who seek them, small bars provide hot snacks, cold drinks and music.

A hike to the caves, coves, bays and beaches adjacent to Sile will stretch the fittest muscles, or alternatively you can take an inexpensive *dolmus* taxi. Outside the resort are secluded places,

most with simple refreshment facilities for those who choose not to take their own picnic. Least energetic of excursions on foot is one to the local lighthouse, Turkey's biggest, dating back to 1858. It is worth the walk for the views from its base and, depending which of the keepers is on duty, you may be able to enjoy a tour of the house and a bird's-eye view of Sile.

For the evenings, beach barbecues where you make your own entertainment are more popular than discothèques, although there are a couple of simple nightspots in the resort.

TRABZON

Trabzon remains the metropolis of the eastern Black Sea coast, and it was here that the last Byzantine emperor watched land and sea for the coming of the Ottoman Turks. The 350-year-old empire of Trebizond, as it was once known, perished on 15 August 1561 after the Turkish Sultan Mehmet II subjected the city to the same total defeat he had inflicted on Constantinople only eight years before.

Enough still remains of the legendary 'towers of Trebizond'

In 13th-century Haghia Sophia, there are many beautiful paintings and gold mosaics on walls and ceiling

to conjure up what the Imperial city must have been like when a Pope of the 14th century wrote ingratiatingly to 'His Magnificent the Emperor of Trebizond'. The city's churches, once the pride and glory of ancient Christendom, were converted to Moslem worship and as a result have survived in better condition. At the Church of the Golden Headed Virgin, now the Ortahisar or Fatih Mosque, the cupola is still plated with gold. Haghia Sophia, the 'Holy Wisdom' of Trebizond, began its life as a church, was converted to a mosque, and is now a museum. It is the best-preserved example of Byzantine architecture on this coast. In the wild mountains steeply rising south of Trabzon, an astonishingly varied fauna persists in the native forest of beech, alder, oak and wild nut trees. Chamois, brown bear, jackal, wild cat, ibex, mountain goat, otter, marten and wild boar are all to be found here (see also page 101).

Tourism bureau: Vilayet Binasi (tel: (031) 35833, 35818, 35830).

HOW TO GET TO THE BLACK SEA COAST

Flights operate from Istanbul and Ankara to Trabzon. By train, the Eastern Express goes from Istanbul via Erzurum to Kars, from where you can continue by bus. There are also bus connections to all provincial centres, while Turkish Maritime Lines operates services to Samsun and Trabzon, a journey that takes two days.

EASTERN TURKEY

The eastern region of Turkey, with the Taurus Mountains in the south and the chain of the Black Sea mountains in the north encircling the Anatolian Plateau to form a mighty, complex mountain range, is a diverse land which differs significantly from the rest of the country.

Visitors here will be amazed by the variety of the landscape: the red ochre plateau of Erzurum; the forests, waterfalls and green pastures of Kars and Agri; the never-melting snow of Mount Agri; the immense Lake Van with its deep blue waters; the torrid plain of High Mesopotamia; and the fertile valleys of the Dicle and Firat.

Historic treasures of the region are likewise full of variety: the astounding sanctuary of Antiochus I, with its colossal statues, at Nemrut Dagi; Byzantine monasteries and churches; mausoleums and caravanserais of the Seljuk period; elegant Ottoman mosques; and hilltop fortresses. As the battlefront of Eastern and Western cultures represented by the Romans and Parthians and the Byzantines and Sassanids, culminating in the final conquest of Anatolia by an Eastern people, the Seljuk Turks, the region has had an active past. In the area where the central steppe gives way to the more mountainous terrain of the east are the important Seljuk centres of Sivas, Divrigi, Eski Malatya and Harput, all of which possess monuments testifying to the brilliant achievements of Seljuk art.

Situated at a height of 1,950m is Erzurum, in which are mosques and mausoleums of the Seljuk and Mongol periods, and the well-preserved walls of a Byzantine fortress. To the north is the much fought-over frontier city of Kars, dominated by a formidable fortress, and nearby are the ruins of 10th-century Ani. Mount Ararat, Turkey's highest mountain, is where Noah's Ark is believed to have come to rest. It is also where history is thought to have begun, and stands as a dividing point between nations and empires. At the base of this mountain is the intriguing 17th-century mosque and palace of Ishak Pasa at Dogubayazit.

On the banks of the immense and beautiful Lake Van is the

Nemrut Dagi is the 2,000-year-old site of a tomb sanctuary, consisting of a series of enormous stone statues

EASTERN TURKEY

city of the same name, with its Urartu citadel dating back to the first millennium BC and mosques and mausoleums of the Seljuk and Ottoman periods.

In the region that was once Upper Mesopotamia in the basin of the Dicle (Tigris) and Firat (Euphrates) are the cities of Diyarbakir, Mardin and Sanliurfa, all former centres of the Hurri-Mitani in the second millennium BC.

Finally, north of Adiyaman in the mountain vastness of the southeast is one of Turkey's most spectacular monuments, the funerary sanctuary of Nemrut Dagi, with its colossal toppled heads of gods, which was erected 2,000 years ago for King Antiochus I.

Life in the region is generally austere, and hotels display little concession towards sophistication, so visitors here must be prepared for simple if not basic standards, and a certain degree of 'roughing' it. It is wise, also, to choose the time of your visit carefully because, due to the altitude and lack of sea influence, the climate of eastern Turkey is one of extremes: dry, hot summers and harsh, severe winters. The climate is even more extreme in the northeast, where winters are long and bitter and the summers merely warm; the southeast boasts scorching summers and short, mild winters.

◆◆◆
DIYARBAKIR

Diyarbakir is one of the most attractive cities in eastern Turkey. Situated on a plateau, it is characterised by triple black basalt walls that encircle the old town, giving it a medieval aspect. These ramparts, which have 16 keeps and five gates, are among the longest in the world. They were built by the Emperor Constantius, son of Constantine the Great, in AD349, have been kept in a constant state of good repair by their various occupiers, and are still in excellent condition along their entire length.

Also of interest in the city is the Ulu Mosque, notable for its

The famous 10th-century Church on the island of Ahtamar, 35km from Van, is the world's finest example of medieval Armenian architecture

original architecture and the amount of ancient materials used in the restoration of the building at various times. The town also boasts an interesting archaeological museum housed in a former theological college, with exhibits covering a period of some 4,000 years.

Hotels
Recommended hotels include the **Demir** and the **Diyarbakir Buyuk Hotel**.
Tourism bureau: Lise Cad. 24/A (tel: (831) 12173, 17840).

◆◆◆

MARDIN
Whereas Diyarbakir is a city of

black appearance due to the basalt used in the old walls, Mardin, which overlooks the vast Mesopotamian plain, is a city of white aspect because of its limestone buildings. Of particular interest in the city is its Roman citadel. This was reputedly impregnable, a claim supported by the fact that neither the Seljuks in the 12th century nor the Mongols in the 13th century managed to capture it. The only one who did was Tamerlane, at the end of the 14th century.

Also of interest to the visitor are various Islamic monuments: the Kasim Pasa Medrese of the 15th century; the Latifiye Mosque and the Ulu Mosque, built in the 11th century by the Seljuks; and the Sultan Isa Medrese, which has a finely-decorated portal.

Four miles (7km) from Mardin, on the road to Akinci, lies the great Jacobite monastery of Deyrulzaferan, while at nearby Kiziltepe is one of the best examples of Seljuk architecture, the 13th-century Ulu Mosque with fine *mihrab* reliefs, and a beautiful portal.

◆◆
LAKE VAN
Lake Van is by far the largest lake in Turkey—five times the size of Lake Geneva, for instance—and is astonishingly beautiful: an inland sea at an altitude of nearly 6,000ft, ringed by the towering mountains of eastern Anatolia. The lake contains sulphur springs at a depth of 300ft along the shore and 600ft in the centre, which give an excessively high salt content to the water, not unlike

the Dead Sea. In winter, navigation of the lake is impossible, fierce and unpredictable storms making it too treacherous. In the summer months, however, the lake is becoming increasingly popular with visitors.

The modern town of Van, which lies about 3 miles (5km) distant inland from the lakeshore, is a delightful place not yet taken over by tourists, although it seems only a matter of time before it will be. For the present, its pleasant restaurants and *lokantas* are refreshingly free from the usual tourist influences. The town of Old Van is situated at the foot of a massive rock platform. Here the citadel, 1¾ miles (3km) west of the new town, dominates the ruins of old churches, of Seljuk and Ottoman mosques, and the homes that are hollowed out of sheer rock. An excellent museum in Van contains fine examples of Urartian artistry and craftsmanship.

At Cavustepe, 22 miles (35km) from Van, there is an important Urartian site with temples, a palace and inscriptions; and in Hosap, 37 miles (60km) distant, there is an interesting 17th-century castle.

◆◆◆
NEMRUT DAGI

Nemrut Dagi is the site of the extraordinary tomb-sanctuary erected 2,000 years ago by King Antiochus I of the Commagenes, the most renowned monarch of a land which encompassed what today is the region of Adiyaman, Maras and Gaziantep.

The monarchs of Commagenes were regarded as gods, and considered themselves as such—and none more so than Antiochus I, who had a group of enormous stone statues seated on thrones erected at the summit of the mountain 'in commemoration of my own glory and of that of the gods'. An act of megalomania, it must have involved an army of slaves toiling for many years to hump the huge stones to the mountain's summit. Over the years the colossal statues, 25–35ft in height, have suffered from the ravages of time, earthquakes and erosion, but the site is still extremely impressive, especially if viewed at either dawn or dusk.

Nemrut Dagi is reached from either the town of Adiyaman, where a jeep and driver can be hired, or the nearer village of Kahta, where accommodation is also available. For those who prefer to make the ascent in late afternoon, primitive lodgings are available on the peak itself.

Tourism bureau: Ataturk Bulv. P.T.T., Yani 41, Adiyaman (tel: (8781) 1008).

HOW TO GET TO EASTERN TURKEY

Turkish Airlines operates frequent services from Istanbul and Ankara to various centres in Eastern Turkey, including Diyarbakir and Van.

By train, the Eastern Express runs between Istanbul–Erzurum–Kars, and also between Istanbul–Mus–Tatvan and on by ferry to Van.

There are also inexpensive bus services from both Istanbul and Ankara to all the principal towns in the region.

PEACE AND QUIET:
Turkey's Countryside and Wildlife

Turkey is steeped in history and rich in wildlife. It has played host to many cultures and civilisations over the last three centuries, and yet much of it is still relatively wild and unspoilt.

Although only 3 per cent of the country lies in Europe, it still boasts most of the species of plant, bird and mammal that are found in adjacent countries like Greece. However, on the Asian side of the Bosphorus, many birds reach their western-most limit, seldom crossing the narrow, watery divide. This strategic position has made the isthmus separating Asia and Europe of immense importance to migrating birds, which pass through Turkey each year in their millions.

The countryside is extraordinarily varied. In spring, the extensive coastlines of the Black and Aegean Seas are a riot of colour; much of the inland area is dominated by the Anatolian plateau, parts of which are high enough to reach the snow line; the extensive wooded slopes are still the haunt of bears and wolves, persecuted to extinction throughout most of the rest of Europe.

Aleppo pines are the most common pines along the Turkish coast. Their shape is usually distinctive

PEACE AND QUIET

Coasts and Sea

The extensive coastline is largely unspoilt, and until comparatively recently was unknown to the majority of tourists. Much of the coast is rugged and mountainous and is cloaked in woodland which drops down to sandy beaches between rocky headlands. Fortunately, some of the best areas have been protected from future development by being given national park status. The Dilek peninsula on the Aegean Sea, which is close to Ephesus and Izmir, is particularly outstanding. Its jagged hills rise from sea level to a height of over 1,200m, providing a wonderful setting for its many archaeological treasures and wildlife. Birds of prey haunt the slopes, and rare and secretive mammals like jackal, striped hyena, wild boar and porcupine are found here. Even leopards are not unknown in Dilek, but to see one of these beautiful animals you will need to be well off the beaten track and extremely lucky.

The national park at Olympos-Bey Daglari protects a stretch of coast running west from the Gulf of Antalya which is also impressively scenic. Mountains rising to over 2,000m and covered in Calabrian pines provide a stunning backdrop for wonderful sandy beaches. From here you may see parties of shearwaters flying by in long formations. Corys are common, and are often joined by the smaller eastern Mediterranean race of the Manx shearwater, known as the Levantine shearwater.

Slender-billed gulls can sometimes be seen around the Turkish coasts

At certain times of the year, gulls can be common around the shores. Little and Mediterranean gulls both sport neat, black hoods and white wings during the breeding season. They are easy to tell apart, however, because the little gull is considerably smaller and has underwings which are almost black. Smaller numbers of slender-billed gulls also pass through the region. They have white heads throughout the year and a close view will reveal their unusual pale eyes.

The coastal scrub can be extremely colourful during April and May, with rock roses and lavenders competing to attract nectar-feeding butterflies such as Amanda's blue and tree grayling. Lizards and snakes, like the fearsome Montpellier snake, rustle gently through the undergrowth, while spur-thighed tortoises are extremely noisy.

In and around Istanbul

The narrow strip of water known as the Bosphorus, now neatly spanned by a bridge, is the dividing line between Asia and Europe. The waters of the Bosphorus run northeast into the the Black Sea and southwest through the Sea of Marmara into the Mediterranean; so, not surprisingly, Istanbul has been an important trading post for centuries. The Bosphorus is also an important route for many seabirds, and incredible numbers of Levantine shearwaters pass through each day.

Istanbul's cosmopolitan atmosphere attracts not only people from far away, but birds as well. Alpine swifts, with their neat black and white plumage, scream overhead, while palm doves peck the ground for seeds and crumbs. These neat little pigeons are widespread in Africa, and Istanbul is their most northerly outpost. Black kites, ubiquitous scavengers of warmer climates, are to be seen everywhere. They will daringly dive down on to the pavement to pick up a scrap of food and often congregate around market places.

Istanbul is also on the migration route for many birds flying from Africa to northern Europe and Asia. Parks and gardens in and around the city provide a welcome stopping-off point for tired migrants and a single tree may hold up to 6 species on a good day during migration time. Spotted and red-breasted flycatchers are common, as well as a variety of warblers, and even golden orioles. They are often joined by Syrian woodpeckers, residents which nest in holes in the trees and

Despite their camouflage, Turkish geckos are often caught

PEACE AND QUIET

Red-footed falcons are among Turkey's most common birds of prey

peck insects from the bark. Travel northwest from the city and you soon reach open country often heavily grazed by goats and sometimes cultivated. Overlooking the fields and scrub, the wires and fences which line the roads provide excellent perches for red-footed falcons, lesser kestrels, shrikes and bee-eaters. Their keen eyes are ever alert for the slightest movement below, which would give away the presence of an insect or a lizard. Turkish geckos are frequent victims and are abundant in the undergrowth, sometimes even venturing inside buildings.

Birds over the Bosphorus

Istanbul's unique position has aided its prosperity throughout the ages, but it has also made it of immense strategic importance to migrating birds. Each spring and autumn, millions of birds pass over the skies of Istanbul on their way to and from their wintering grounds in Africa. The reason for the concentration of large birds of prey and storks through the region is simple. Most large birds migrate by day, using thermals to give them lift and assist their passage, and so avoid crossing seas and oceans wherever possible, because very little heat rises off the water. The narrow isthmus on which Istanbul is sited effectively provides a land bridge between the Mediterranean and the Black Sea. The only thing standing in the way of the birds' migration route is the narrow strip of water called the Bosphorus, and so every morning in spring and autumn birds congregate in the skies over the hills around the Bosphorus, gathering enough

height to glide over the water.
The thousands of birds which
pass through each day provide a
memorable spectacle.
Although you can witness
impressive migration almost
anywhere around Istanbul, the
Camlica hills on the Asiatic side
of the Bosphorus are generally
considered to give the best
vantage point. From March until
May the skies are full of Levant
sparrowhawks, honey buzzards,
black kites and lesser-spotted
eagles. Their numbers are
supplemented by red-footed
falcons, lesser kestrels, booted
eagles and harriers, and both
white and black storks are a
daily feature, sometimes
numbering into the thousands.
The same spectacle can be
witnessed in the autumn, from
August until October, but at this
season, of course, the migration
is in the other direction.
Although autumn migration is
perhaps not as concentrated as
that in spring, the young birds of
that year swell the numbers to
unbelievable proportions.
If possible, time your arrival on
the Camlica hills to just after
dawn. At first the only birds
around will be the local resident
species and a few smaller
migrants, but as the sun's rays
warm the ground, thermals will
build up and gradually storks
and eagles will take to the air in
ever-increasing numbers.

Hills and Mountains
Much of the central region of
Turkey is dominated by the hilly
Anatolian plateau which still
holds vast tracts of wild and
unspoilt country. Much of the
land is more than 1,000m above

sea level and in places it rises
much higher. Bolkar Dag, east of
Antalya, rises to over 3,300m
(10,800ft), while Mount Ararat or
Agri, widely held to be the
resting place of Noah's Ark,
reaches over 5,200m (17,000ft) on
the Russian border.
Many of the more exciting areas
are to all intents and purposes
inaccessible. However, areas
like Kovada Lake at the western
end of the Taurus Mountain
range have received national
park status to protect them.
Although close to the sea, the
wooded slopes make a
refreshing change from the
coast, and the oaks and
Calabrian pines provide shelter
for red and roe deer, wild boar
and wolves. Although nearly
hunted to extinction, small
numbers of European brown
bears survive here and in other
remote regions. Sadly, a few are
still trained and kept as 'dancing
bears', a degrading occupation
for one of Europe's most
magnificent animals.
The open slopes are the haunts
of golden eagles, which glide
effortlessly on their immense
wings over the broken terrain.
Although they will feed on
carrion, they are adept at
hunting for themselves, and
chukars (a species of partridge)
are an important part of their
diet. Vultures, on the other hand,
feed almost exclusively on
animal remains and seldom kill
anything for themselves. Griffon,
black and Egyptian vultures, are
all likely to be seen in the wilder
regions and are sometimes
joined by the majestic
lammergeier, with its long
tapering wings.

PEACE AND QUIET

Rocky gullies and gorges are the favoured nesting sites for rock thrushes and blue rock thrushes, the latter with its slaty-blue plumage looking dull in comparison to the gaudy male rock thrush. Despite its vivid colours, the rock thrush is often not spotted until it flies, when its white rump is conspicuous. In the highest and most inaccessible gorges, close to the snow line, the lucky visitor may see Caspian snowcocks, a speciality of the region. These large, turkey-like birds are rather wary of people and seldom venture below 2,000m (6,500ft) in the summer. When disturbed, they characteristically either run uphill or fly downhill to escape danger.

European brown bears are still found in small numbers in prime woodland

Woodlands

Woodlands remain widespread in Turkey and provide cool shade for both walker and wildlife. In central areas of Turkey especially, the forests help moderate the extremes in temperature, remaining cool in summer and providing shelter in winter. Coastal areas and the lower slopes of the hills often have deciduous trees such as oak, chestnut, plane and beech, while pines and firs prefer the higher reaches.

Just outside Istanbul, on the European side of the Bosphorus, lies the Belgrade Forest, a largely deciduous area of oak and ash. Bright yellow and orange Cleopatra butterflies flit along the glades, while Hungarian gliders live up to their name and race along. In spring, the trees come alive with a chorus of nightingales, blackcaps and golden orioles, but hearing them will prove much easier than seeing them as they flit through the dappled leaf canopy.

Honey buzzards are secretive nesters in the highest branches of the trees. They are easiest to see early in the season, just after their arrival from Africa, when they soar overhead in display flights showing their characteristic barred underwings. As their name implies, their favourite food is to be found in the underground nests of wild bees and wasps. You may spot the tell-tale excavations along forest rides where the nests have been raided, but it is not the honey that the buzzards consume, but insect larvae. In the skies above

Dense woodland is home to the Syrian woodpecker

the woods, they are often joined by hobbies acrobatically catching insects on the wing. The mountains of the Taurus range on Turkey's southern coast, as well as the Anatolian plateau, still support vast areas of prime woodland, despite forest clearance and damage by grazing animals. Yedigoller, northwest of Ankara, is a national park containing both deciduous and coniferous woodland between 700 and 1,500m (5,000ft) above sea level. Deer and wild boar roam these woods and wolves and brown bears occur in small numbers. Middle-spotted and Syrian woodpeckers nest and feed in the lower branches of the trees, while overhead, short-toed eagles circle in the thermals. These pale birds of prey specialise in catching reptiles and sometimes one is seen flying with a lifeless snake in its talons.

Agricultural Land

Farmland in Turkey is a botanist's delight. Because the farming is less intensive and herbicides seldom used, the so-called cornfield 'weeds', now a thing of the past in many other countries, abound. Throughout the spring and summer, corn marigolds, mayweeds, cornflowers, poppies, pheasant's eye and borage offer a whole spectrum of colours and are enthusiastically visited by numerous bees and butterflies. If there are orchards nearby, then black-veined whites and scarce swallowtails, butterflies whose caterpillars feed on the leaves of fruit trees, will be frequent and conspicuous visitors.

Olives are commonly grown in Turkey, and ancient groves of gnarled and twisted trees are a familiar sight. Their leaves provide shade and shelter for olive tree and olivaceous warblers, large birds by the standards of other warblers, with loud, harsh alarm calls and songs. Masked shrikes are also frequent in olive groves and orchards, their song and alarm calls sounding remarkably similar to those of the warblers. These elegant, insectivorous birds have the most restricted distribution of all the Eurasian shrikes and Turkey is probably the best country anywhere to search for them.

Olive groves and orchards are often grazed by goats, which soon create a disturbed and dusty soil. Although this may not suit many animals and plants, it is very much to the liking of resident and migrant pipits and larks. The sandy-coloured tawny

PEACE AND QUIET

A typical small Turkish farm, with a patchwork of habitats

pipit feeds alongside crested and short-toed larks which search for small insects and seeds among the broken soil. Wherever there are overhead wires in Turkey you will find birds perching on them. Colourful bee-eaters and bright blue rollers use these man-made lookouts to scan the ground below for insects and other small animals. Bee-eaters prefer to catch bees and dragonflies in flight, while rollers drop to the ground to secure grasshoppers or even small lizards. They are often joined on the wires by black-headed buntings, bright yellow birds with smart, black caps which use the perches to advertise their territories with their repetitive songs.

Open Country

Centuries of woodland clearance and grazing by goats have produced tracts of open, barren country. For most of the year the land is a uniform sandy brown, with the dried remains of plants and only the occasional evergreen shrub like kermes oak to break the monotony. However, for a couple of months in spring, the fields come alive with colourful plants such as asphodel, tassel hyacinths and a whole range of orchids, and tree grayling and Amanda's blue butterflies feast on the nectar. Spring is also the time when reptiles are at their most conspicuous. Wall lizards bask in the early morning sun and spur-thighed tortoises noisily plod through the vegetation. Where the soil is light and sandy, the females lay their eggs in excavated pits, leaving them to incubate in the warm soil. Dry, barren fields are the favoured haunt of wheatears. These alert little birds all share the same upright stance as they hop along the ground and a conspicuous white rump when they fly. Several species pass through Turkey on migration but two commonly stay to breed in these open habitats. Black-eared wheatears have a pale body with contrasting black wings and cheeks, and some adult males even have a black throat making them look most distinguished.

The isabelline wheatear, which is a pale, uniform sandy colour all over and has longer legs than other wheatears, is also common in Asiatic Turkey, although it is almost unknown on the other side of the Bosphorus. Like its black-eared relative, it has to keep a wary eye open for predators such as the Levant sparrowhawk, which flies low over the ground and surprises its quarry.

In wilder, more remote areas, jackals still roam the open country. Although wisely distrustful of man, they can sometimes be seen trotting in the distance and in the evenings, their long, drawn-out howls a reminder of the untamed nature of much of Turkey. Long-legged buzzards also populate this bleak terrain, rising on thermals above rocky outcrops and cliffs. They share the air with many other similar-sized birds of prey but they are the only species with an unbarred, buff tail. On the ground below, red-fronted serins, with their dark heads and red crowns, feed on scrubby hillsides. Both this species and the long-legged buzzard are truly Asiatic and are almost unknown in Europe.

Lakes and Marshes

On the northwest coast of Asiatic Turkey there are large lakes which lie within easy reach of Istanbul. The most westerly of these is Lake Manyas, south of Bandirma, and its northeast shore is now a national park. The lake is low-lying, being only 10m above sea level, and has extensive reedbeds with willow scrub, which support vast numbers of breeding herons and egrets. Among the trees, mixed colonies of pygmy cormorant, spoonbill and glossy ibis nest in May and June. The ibises are often seen probing the muddy margins in search of food; in flight, they have a conspicuously bulbous head.

Lake Iznik, southwest of Izmir, is also rich in bird life and this spectacle is improved by the stunning, mountainous backdrop. In the extensive reedbeds, tree frogs keep up an all-day chorus, seemingly oblivious to the heat of the sun. Deep in the cover of the reeds, purple herons and little bitterns rear their young, but are seldom seen except when in flight. Fish are abundant in the shallow

Marshes and low-lying land are home to many reptiles, including the painted frog

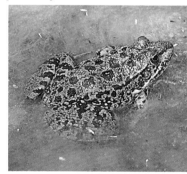

waters and, consequently, most of the larger birds feed almost exclusively on them. In the open water, flocks of white and Dalmatian pelicans glide gracefully, sometimes scooping the water with their capacious beaks.

Lying so close to the migration route through the Bosphorus and close to the sea, the lakes of northwest Turkey are important stopping-off points for migrants. In the spring, Caspian and white-winged black terns boost the numbers of breeding whiskered terns, and many migrant storks drop in to feed for a day or two. In the autumn, however, after the hot summer has dried extensive muddy margins, the lakes become extremely attractive to migrant waders. Ruffs, little stints, wood sandpipers and pratincoles supplement the numbers of breeding black-winged stilts and spur-winged plovers.

Further around the coast, rivers that run down to the sea often create marshes and pools. Although smaller in scale than the lakes near Istanbul, they can nevertheless hold considerable wildlife interest. Painted frogs and tree frogs are sometimes found in such places, attracting herons and egrets if the site is undisturbed, and during spring and autumn, migrants can drop in at any time.

Uludag National Park

Lying to the south of the town of Bursa in northern Asiatiç Turkey, the Uludag National Park embraces the southern slopes of Mount Uludag. This rises from land below 500m to the summit at over 2,500m (8,200ft) above sea level, but fortunately a road zig-zags its way up the slope. As an added bonus, the traveller passes through all the major environmental zones found in Turkey, from Mediterranean maquis all the way to the snow line.

On the lower slopes and on the fringes of cultivated areas, rock roses, lavenders and kermes oak, the latter with leaves like miniature holly, brighten the landscape wherever the goats have failed to graze. Colourful members of the bee orchid family, with their furry, chestnut and pink flowers, grow out of even the barest earth, and insects such as the mantis fly throng through the air. These curious insects are particularly active at dusk and are easily recognised by their lazy flight and elegant, streamer-like hind wings. Syrian woodpeckers inspect the bark of the trees and sometimes even visit telegraph poles, while red-backed shrikes and cirl buntings nest in the scrubby undergrowth.

As the road climbs, it passes through varied woodland containing beech, laurel, chestnut, firs and pines. This mixture of tree species attracts a variety of woodland birds, from warblers to black woodpeckers. Birds of prey nest in the high tree canopies and soar overhead during the heat of the day. The woods also provide a safe haven for mammals like brown bear, wild boar, jackal and wolf, who do not often venture out of cover before nightfall.

Uludag is also a ski resort during the winter, and near the summit,

The elegant, adult mantis fly is a resident of rocky hillsides and abandoned farmland

hotels, ski lifts and cable railways bear witness to its popularity. Despite this disturbance, however, inaccessible crags and gullies provide feeding areas and nesting sites for rock thrushes and rock sparrows, while shore larks and alpine accentors are often seen.

The skies over the mountain are the realm of vultures and eagles. Griffon vultures rise on the first thermals of the day and their broad wings can keep them aloft for hours on end. Golden and Bonelli's eagles are also frequently seen, the latter with a remarkably quick turn of speed when needed.

Turtles

Turkey is one of the last countries bordering the Mediterranean which still supports a mainland breeding population of loggerhead turtles.

Disturbance and tourist development have caused them to desert all but the most remote island sites elsewhere in Europe; and with Turkey's ever-growing tourist industry, how long will they remain here?

The loggerhead turtles' dilemma is that they traditionally lay their eggs on the same sandy beaches that have recently become so attractive to people. Although they visit the sites at night, when the beaches are comparatively deserted by tourists, inconsiderate behaviour can cause them to retreat back to the water without laying their eggs, never to return to the beach again. The eggs, which are left to incubate in the sand for nearly two months, are also vulnerable to digging and trampling, and if the turtles are to survive they must be given precedence over people in certain critical sites. The beach at Dalyan, near Fethiye in southwest Turkey, is now the only major nesting beach in the country and it is still

PEACE AND QUIET

Turtles are pitifully vulnerable when on land

visited by nearly 300 animals a year. It ranks as the second most important site, after the Greek island of Zakynthos, in the whole of the Mediterranean. Conservation bodies have managed to persuade the Turkish authorities that this site is of such importance that it must be saved, and the beach and its surroundings have recently been declared a national conservation area. Hopefully, the authorities will soon realise that there is also money to be made from the presence of the turtles: with careful guidance and supervision, large numbers of people can watch these magnificent animals laying their eggs, without causing them undue distress.

During the egg-laying season turtles are often seen off shore in the bays and coves which adorn the Turkish coast, and to see them swimming in the sea is to see them in their element. On land their movements are woefully inadequate and they are barely able to haul their great shells up the beaches. At sea, however, they literally 'fly' through the water and are as graceful as any bird in flight, their long, paddle-like flippers powering them along.

The Waldrapp

The small town of Birecik, which lies on the River Euphrates close to the Syrian border, is host to the last remaining site, not only in Turkey but also in Eurasia, for the waldrapp or bald ibis. The colony, which now only nests on the rock faces surrounded by the village itself, is in great danger of extinction.

Waldrapps spend the spring in and around Birecik, feeding in the few remaining marshy meadows in the vicinity of the village and nesting on rock ledges. After July, however, they disperse to their wintering grounds in the Middle East and north Africa.

Formerly threatened by hunting and now by the use of pesticides and changes in land use, the population in Birecik had dwindled to 13 birds by 1984. A similar pattern of decline has occurred in the waldrapp's other colonies in Morocco and Algeria, with the entire population being no more than a few hundred strong, and its prospects seem bleak. Perhaps the only long-term future for this bizarre bird, which was once recorded in ancient Egyptian hieroglyphics, is in captivity, where it breeds with some success.

FOOD AND DRINK

It is worth going to Turkey just to eat. The food, particularly fruit and vegetables, is fresh and nutritious, with large, healthy amounts of grains and pulses used in the dishes, often topped with delicious creamy yoghurt. Nor do you need a real grasp of the Turkish language to appreciate the cuisine; in many of the simpler establishments it is sufficient simply to point to what you want if it is on display, or even venture into the kitchen to make your selection if it is not. Lamb is the basic meat of Turkish cooking whether in casseroles or as the famous *sis kebab*—charcoal grilled on a skewer—or *doner kebabs* served in pitta bread.

Fish, which is priced in restaurants according to individual size, is usually fresh from the day's catch. *Barbunya* (red mullet), *kilic baligi* (swordfish), *lufer* (blue-fish), *kalkan* (turbot) and *levrek* (bass) are among the most tasty. The best known *meze* or hors d'œuvres are *dolma*, vegetables such as peppers, aubergines, vine leaves and cabbage leaves stuffed with rice, pine nuts and currants. *Zeytinyagli*, dishes of cold vegetables in olive oil, include *imam bayildi*, meaning 'the priest fainted', a dish of

As fresh as they come: fish is cooked before it is even landed at the quayside in Istanbul

aubergines stuffed with fried tomatoes, onions and garlic. *Boreks* are delicious small pies of filo or flaky pastry filled with meat or cheese.

Desserts are usually based on milk, such as *sutlac* (rice pudding), or pastries soaked in syrup, like *baklava* (flaky pastry stuffed with nuts in syrup) and *tel kadayif*, shredded wheat with nuts and syrup. And if other sweet goodies such as *hanim gobegi* (lady's navel), and *dilber dudagi* (lips of a beauty) don't tempt, there are fresh grapes, peaches, apricots, figs or a slice of melon to finish your meal.

At street corners you will encounter Turkish youths selling circular bread rolls called *simit*, which are covered with sesame seeds; sandwich salesmen making up their products on the spot; and other vendors selling corn-on-the-cob and a great variety of Turkish pastries.

Among alcoholic drinks are the light Turkish beer, excellent red and white wines and the national drink *raki*, which clouds when water is added, giving it the name 'lion's milk'.

Popular non-alcoholic drinks include *ayran*, a mixture of yoghurt, water and a pinch of salt, and fresh fruit juices.

SHOPPING

Virtually every city, town and holiday resort in Turkey offers a good range of shopping possibilities, from modern stores and boutiques to colourful bazaars and bustling markets brimming with Turkish crafts, where bargaining is the order of the day. Copper and brassware, meershaum pipes, alabaster and onyx ware all make good souvenirs; porcelain goods and hand-painted ceramics are also good value, with beautifully decorated plates and ornamental tiles in all sizes. But perhaps the intricately-patterned carpets are the most evocative mementoes of Turkey. In addition to carpets there are boldly patterned *kilims* (woven rugs), *cicims* (embroidered rugs) and rugs of angora goat hair.

Leather goods, especially coats and jackets, are inexpensive, although of wildly varying quality, and light cotton fabrics fashioned into stylish European designs are another good buy. Especially popular with visitors are tee shirts imitating designer labels.

Gold and silver jewellery is often sold according to weight rather than design, and you can choose from rings and bracelets with precious or semi-precious stones, especially turquoise, and traditional jewellery ornamented with amber and agate.

ACCOMMODATION

Tourism is fairly new to Turkey and consequently, although the building of hotels, holiday villages and self-catering apartments is proceeding apace, much of the existing accommodation is not of the same standard that visitors may have become used to in more developed holiday destinations. Generally speaking, older hotels and *pensions* will typically have traditional-style heavy furniture, no shower tray in some of the bathrooms—just a hole in the floor—and be fairly spartan if not extremely basic. Three-and four-bedded rooms in hotels are usually twin-bedded rooms with extra beds, often of the folding kind, and may therefore be rather cramped. Nor are beds always interior sprung divans; they may be built-in platform beds or a mattress on a wire base.

NIGHTLIFE

Turkey is not noted for its pulsating nightlife, but the growth in tourism in recent years has seen discos opening up in many of the major holiday resorts to cater for younger holiday-makers, and a proliferation of 'folklore' evenings complete with belly dancing. Istanbul and Ankara both offer a good selection of nightclubs serving excellent food accompanied by varied entertainment. Otherwise, night-time activities tend to centre on *al fresco* dining, perhaps accompanied by Turkish musicians.

HOW TO BE A LOCAL

If you want to be a local you need to know what is going on, and for this a newspaper detailing daily events is essential. *The Turkish Daily News*, the country's leading English language newspaper is to be recommended. A few guidelines as to local customs will perhaps be useful. Hospitality is important to the Turkish people. The normal form of greeting is to shake hands. Visitors should always respect Islamic customs if they do not wish to offend. Informal wear is acceptable, but scanty beachwear should be confined

Part of the annual festival in Ephesus takes place in the ancient Grand Theatre, which once seated 25,000

to the beach or poolside. It would also be seen as courteous if during the time of Ramadan, visitors were to refrain from drinking alcohol. Smoking is widely accepted, but it is prohibited in cinemas, theatres, city buses and shared taxis (*dolmus*). The Moslem place of worship, the mosque, is available to all visitors, but be sure to enter in stockinged feet or wearing the felt overshoes left outside the mosque. To be truly accepted as a local, you must be able to bargain well. Bargaining is a game enjoyed by the Turks and no-one will be offended if there is no deal at the end.

FESTIVALS, FAIRS AND SPECIAL EVENTS
January
Camel Wrestling Festival, Selcuk
April–May
International Arts Festival, Ankara
Ephesus Festival, Selcuk
May
International Music & Folklore Festival, Silifke
June
Ataturk Culture & Arts Week, Amasya
Marmaris Festival
Bergama Festival
Cesme Sea Festival
Ilhara Tourism & Culture Festival, Aksaray
June–July
International Istanbul Arts & Culture Festival
Grease Wrestling, Edirne
International Festival, Izmir
July
International Culture & Arts Festival, Bursa
International Folklore Festival, Samsun
Ceramics Festival, Kutahya

August
Troy Festival, Canakkale
September–October
International Fair & Festival, Mersin
International Mediterranean Song Festival, Antalya
December
St Nicholas Festival, Demre
Mevlana Commemoration Ceremony, Konya

CLIMATE
Turkey is a vast country, and climatic conditions vary enormously. The Mediterranean and Aegean coasts enjoy the most agreeable year-round weather, but visitors should be prepared for extreme heat in the height of the summer, and not over-do the sunbathing in the early stages. The Mediterranean tends to be even hotter and more humid than the Aegean. The Black Sea region is cooler, and rainier, while visits to Eastern Turkey are not recommended in winter because of the extreme cold.

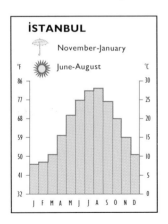

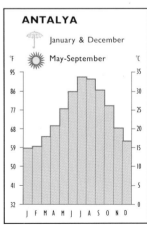

DIRECTORY

Arriving

By Air

Many international airlines operate direct scheduled services to Istanbul and Ankara, from where there are frequent connections to Turkey's principal holiday centres. In addition, an increasing number of charter flights are being operated to Turkey, especially to the airports of Izmir, Dalaman and Antalya, serving the fast-expanding holiday resorts on the Aegean and Mediterranean coasts.

By Sea

In addition to the numerous cruises in the Mediterranean, several foreign shipping companies have regular services to the ports of Istanbul, Izmir, Kusadasi and Bodrum.

Car ferries: Turkish Maritime Lines sails regularly from 1 April to October. The Mersin–Magosa (Turkish Republic of Northern Cyprus) line runs three times a week year-round. There are also services to Cyprus from Tasucu, near Silifke.

By Rail

There are regular train services to Istanbul from principal European cities – Paris, Venice and Munich, for example. Internally, there is an efficient train network linking all parts of the country; so, with planning, it is perfectly possible to arrive in Turkey by train.

By Road

Driving to Turkey from most European countries is a daunting undertaking, not only lengthy but

Popular Olu Deniz Bay has a spectacular backdrop

You may not have seen before a baker's boy quite like this one selling his wares outside a Konya mosque

involving the awful roads of Yugoslavia. There are two principal routes:-
Northern Route: either: (1) Nuremberg, Linz, Vienna, Budapest, Belgrade; or (2) Stuttgart, Munich, Salzburg, Ljubliana, Zagreb, Belgrade; and from Belgrade to Nis, Sofia, Edirne and Istanbul.
Southern route: Geneva, Venice, Ljubliana, Belgrade, Sofia, Istanbul. Driving south from Munich you can use the car ferry service to Istanbul, Izmir and Kusadasi.

Baths

Because of the emphasis placed on cleanliness by Islam, there have been public bath houses (*hamam*) in Turkey since medieval times. There are separate baths for men and women, or when there is only one bath house in town, different days are allocated to men and women. After entering the

hamam and leaving your clothes in a cubicle, you proceed, wrapped in a towel (*pestemal*) to a large heated stone where you are rubbed down by a bath attendant. If the heat proves too much there is a cooler room where you can lie for a while. Many of the baths are in buildings of considerable architectural interest.

Car Breakdown—Repairs and Accidents

In case of an accident

Whether or not anyone is injured, the police should be notified as a report is essential. If you hold a credit cheque from your own automobile association, the Turkish Touring and Automobile Association (*Turkiye Turing ve Otomobil Kurumu*) will carry out necessary repairs and forward the bill in Swiss Francs to your own country.
If you possess an AIT or an FIA assistance booklet, the Turkish Touring and Automobile Association will bear the cost of transporting your damaged vehicle from the scene of the accident to the Customs and thence to your home.
If it is necessary to leave a vehicle in Turkey after an accident for eventual collection, the vehicle must be delivered to a Customs Office so that its endorsement on your passport may be deleted. Without this deletion it is not possible to leave the country. When leaving a vehicle at the Customs, it should be made clear that this is a temporary measure, since any vehicle not claimed within three months is considered to have been abandoned.

If your vehicle is totally wrecked and you wish to abandon it in Turkey, it should be taken to the nearest Customs Office. If there is not one nearby, then you should contact the local administrative authority (*Mulki Amirlik*) to arrange for the vehicle to be sent to a Customs Office. The latter will then cancel the endorsement of the vehicle in your passport and you will be free to leave Turkey. If your vehicle is stolen it is necessary to obtain a certificate from the governor of the province (*Vali*), again so that the vehicle's endorsement in your passport can be cancelled before you leave the country.

Repairs
There are numerous repair garages in towns (usually grouped along special streets) and along principal highways. Spare parts for the most common makes of cars are usually fairly easily available.
In addition, assistance can be sought from the Touring and Automobile Association: Istanbul head office (tel: 1467090, 5216588); Edirne frontier office (tel: 03 Kapikule/34); Ankara office (tel: 1317649).

Car Hire
Car hire in Turkey is not cheap, and many of the vehicles offered for rent are of dubious standard. Best bets are probably Hertz, Avis, Budget and Europcar which are extending their outlets throughout the country to embrace most of the principal airports, cities and holiday resorts. It is important, also, to consider that the final cost may be higher than originally

estimated, since a ten per cent tax is added to the bill. You will need to show your driving licence, of course, and an international licence could be useful, though not obligatory.

Chemist – see Health

Crime
In rural areas, law and order are upheld not by the police—who operate in plain clothes— but by armed and uniformed members of the *jandarma*, a section of the Army. Although disconcerting to first-time visitors, their visibility has the effect of keeping trouble to a minimum. Police operate, as usual, in towns and cities. The one cardinal rule, of course, is not to import drugs into Turkey, or take them while there. Likewise, though pick-pocketing, bag snatching and mugging are practically unheard of in Turkey, it is still sensible to take the precaution of not carrying all your valuables and travel documents with you while sightseeing.

Customs Regulations
Foreign tourists may take into Turkey duty-free: personal effects; medical items; one camera with up to 10 rolls of film; 400 cigarettes or 50 cigars or 500g tobacco (an additional 600 cigarettes, 100 cigars or 500g tobacco may be imported if purchased at the Turkish duty-free shops on arrival); 1kg coffee; 1.5kg instant coffee; 1kg chocolate; 5 (100cc) or 7 (70cc) bottles of alcohol; 5 bottles of perfume. Valuable items should be registered in the owner's passport for control on exit. The bringing into the country or use

of narcotics is strictly forbidden, and subject to heavy penalities. On exit, the export of antiquities is forbidden.

Domestic travel

Air
There are flights from Istanbul and Ankara to Adana, Antalya, Dalaman, Diyarbakir, Erzurum, Gaziantep, Izmir, Kayseri, Konya, Malatya, Sivas, Trabzon, Van.

Sea
Turkish Maritime Lines operates year-round car and passenger ferry services from Istanbul to Izmir and on the Black Sea route to Samsun and Trabzon.

Rail
Within Turkey, rail services connect major cities, but it is usually a lot quicker by bus. Trains have couchettes and restaurant cars offering first and second class service. In Istanbul eastbound trains leave from Haydarpasa Station on the Asian side.

Buses
Inter-City Coaches: private companies provide an extensive network of inexpensive services which run day and night between all Turkish cities. Services are frequent, though on many routes there is no set timetable. Coaches depart from the bus station (*otogar*) in large towns and from the centre of town in smaller places.

Taxis
Taxis are numerous in all Turkish cities and are recognisable by their illuminated taxi signs. The fare shown on the meter is according to kilometres travelled. The *dolmus* is a

A million or so Turks are still nomadic, especially in summer; these nomads have camped in the mountains by Lake Van in eastern Turkey near the Iranian border

shared taxi which follows specific routes within large cities, to suburbs, airports and within popular holiday resorts.

Cars
Cars, minibuses, caravans, towed sea craft and motorcycles can be taken into Turkey for up to three months without a Carnet de Passage or triptique. The vehicle is simply registered in the owner's passport and this registration is cancelled when the owner leaves the country. For stays longer than three months it is necessary to apply to the Turkish Touring and Automobile Association for a triptique; otherwise the vehicle must leave and re-enter the country after three months. If you

wish to visit another country from Turkey without your car, you should take the vehicle to the nearest Customs Authority (*Gumruk Mudurlugu*) so that the registration of the car in your passport can be cancelled.

Traffic circulation: Traffic circulates on the right and the Turkish Highway Code is similar to those of European countries. Outside the cities, traffic moves comparatively freely, the Istanbul–Ankara highway being the only one on which it is consistently extremely heavy. There is a 30mph (50kph) speed limit in urban centres and a 56mph (90kph) limit outside urban centres.

Petrol: Petrol prices are below most European ones, though there are slight variations depending on the nearness of a filling station to a refinery. The brands of petrol available are: Petrol Ofisi, Turk Petrol, BP, Mobil and Shell. 'Super' grades of petrol can be found all over the country save in the most isolated parts. Filling stations are well distributed, and those on the main highways often have service stations and restaurants attached, and are open 24hrs.

Road signs: Turkish road signs conform to the International Protocol on Road Signs. Archaeological and historical sites are indicated by yellow signposts.

Insurance: A motorist should have either:-

a) Green Card international insurance endorsed for Turkish territory both Europe and Asia, or

b) Turkish third party insurance, which can be obtained from any of the insurance agencies at the frontier posts.

Electricity
The standard voltage in Turkey is 220 volts AC, and the sockets are generally of the Continental two-pronged round-pin variety, so adaptors may be necessary if you want to use a hairdryer or electric razor.

Emergency
See **Health** for hospital numbers

Embassies
Britain: Embassy—Sehit Ersan Caddesi 46/A, Cankaya, Ankara (tel: (4) 1274310); Consulate—Mesrutiyet Caddesi 34, Tepebasi, Istanbul (tel: (1) 1447540).

United States: Embassy—Ataturk Bulvari 110, Cankaya, Ankara (tel: (4) 1265470); Consulate—Mesrutiyet Caddesi 104, Tepebasi, Istanbul (tel: (1) 1513602).

DIRECTORY

Canada: Nenehatun Caddesi 75, Gaziosmanpasa, Ankara (tel: (4) 1275803).
Australia: Nenehatun Caddesi 83, Gaziosmanpasa, Ankara (tel: (4) 1286715).

Health

No vaccinations are normally required by the Turkish authorities, though some doctors do advise vaccination against diseases such as typhoid, tetanus, polio and hepatitis A for anyone visiting foreign countries. It is best to check with your own doctor. It is also advisable to take out medical insurance and ensure that, if you intend visiting both the European and Asian sections of Turkey, the policy covers both areas.

Visitors unaccustomed to foreign food can sometimes experience stomach upsets, so it is useful to take appropriate medication with you. Alternatively, this can be obtained from Turkish chemist shops (*eczane*) which stock a good range of medications to cure most ailments.

Tap water is generally safe, but bottled water is cheap and always a wiser option.

In emergencies, contact the American Hospital in Istanbul, Guzelbahce Sokagi 20, Nisantasi (tel: (1) 0314050), or the medical centre attached to the University of Hacettepe in Ankara (tel: (4) 324 2240).

Holidays
Public:

1 January	New Year's Day
23 April	National Independence and Children's Day
19 May	Ataturk Commemoration and Youth and Sports Day
30 August	Victory Day
29 October	Republic Day

Religious: There are two religious holidays celebrated in Turkey. The first is the three-day 'Seker Bayrami' (Candy Festival), when sweets are eaten to mark the end of the fast of Ramazan. The second is the four-day 'Kurban Bayrami' (Festival of Sacrifice) when sacrificial sheep are slaughtered and their meat distributed to the poor. The dates of these festivals change according to the Moslem calendar and during the festivals shops and government offices are closed.

Money Matters

The monetary system is the Turkish Lira (L). Coins in circulation are of 5, 10, 25, 50 and 100 Lira, and banknotes in denominations of L 10, 20, 50, 100, 500, 1000, 5000, 10,000 and 20,000.

There are no restrictions on the amount of foreign currency or Turkish Lira that can be taken into Turkey, but not more than US$1,000-worth of Turkish currency may be taken out of the country. Up to the equivalent of US$3,000 in foreign currency may be exported.

Exchange slips: Currency exchange receipts should be kept for reconverting Turkish Lira into foreign currency on departure, and also as proof that any large purchase, such as a carpet, has been bought with legally exchanged foreign currency.

Credit cards: Most international credit cards are becoming more widely accepted in the larger cities and resorts, but do not depend on them. They are unlikely to be used in smaller restaurants or villages, for instance, so it is advisable to take travellers' cheques, Eurocheques or foreign currency which can be easily cashed at any bank.

Banks: Open weekdays 08.30–12.00hrs and 13.30–17.00hrs. Closed on Saturdays, Sundays and public holidays.

Opening Times

Government offices: 08.30–12.30hrs; 13.30–17.30hrs. Closed Saturdays and Sundays

Shops: 09.30–13.00hrs; 14.00–19.00hrs. Closed Sundays. Covered Bazaar, Istanbul: 08.30–19.00hrs. Closed Sundays.

Museums: Most Turkish museums are open every day of the week, except Mondays, but it would be wise to check first. Palaces are open every day except Mondays and Thursdays. The Topkapi Palace Museum in Istanbul shuts on Tuesdays.

Personal Safety

Apart from the possibility of stomach upsets brought on by eating unfamiliar food, there is not much to worry about when travelling in Turkey. Mosquitoes can be a nuisance—it's wise to take repellants with you because they are not easily obtainable on the spot—and you should be wary of snakes, some poisonous, when scrambling among unexcavated ruins.

Pharmacist—see Health

Police—see Crime

An enterprising shoe-shine man and his attractive stall, Istanbul

Post & Telephone

Turkish post offices are easily recognisable by their yellow 'PTT' signs. Major post offices are open 08.00–24.00hrs Monday–Saturday and 09.00–19.00hrs, Sunday.

Poste restante letters should be addressed 'posterestant' to the central post office 'Merkez Postanesu' in the town or holiday resort of your choice. It is only necessary to produce means of identification when collecting your mail.

Phone calls: For local inter-city and international calls, tokens—*jetons*—should be obtained. Telephone cards are also available. To make an international call, first dial 9 then, after a new tone, 9 again. Then dial the full number.

Student and Youth Travel

All young people and students travelling through the member organisations of BITS, FIYTO and ISTC, and holding ISIC,

DIRECTORY

Ancient and modern – olives and communications spheres at Mardin

INTERAIL, BIGE and YIEE cards of these organisations, can make use of some of the excellent hostels and centres located in various parts of Turkey. These include:-

Topkapi Ataturk Student Centre, Londra Asfalti, Cevizlibag Duragi, Topkapi, Istanbul (tel: (1) 5820461) (directorate); 5820455 (operator). 750 beds.

Kadirga Student Hostel, Comertler Sokak No 6, Kumpapi, Istanbul (tel: (1) 5270218) (directorate), 5282480 (operator). 500 beds.

Intepe Youth and Boy Scout Hostel, Guzelyali Mevkii, Tusan Moteli Yani, Guzelyali 16–26, Canakkale.

Hasanaga Youth and Boy Scout Hostel, Kucuk Kumla/Gemlik (tel: 289 Kumla, Bursa).

Cumhuriyet Youth Hostel, Cebeci, Ankara (tel: (4) 32201597) (directorate), 3193634 (operator). 1058 beds.

Ataturk Student Hostel Inciralti, 1888 Sok, No 4 Inciralti, Izmir (tel: (51) 152980/155077). 750 beds.

Student reductions: Some Turkish organisations and companies, such as Turkish Airlines, recognise the ISTC card and accordingly grant reductions to holders. Turkish Maritime Lines and Turkish railways, for instance, grant 10 per cent reductions; cinemas and concert halls 50 per cent reductions; and a similar discount applies on many long-distance coach trips.

Time

Turkish time is two hours ahead of GMT, and seven hours ahead of US Eastern Standard Time.

Tipping
Although tipping is not considered obligatory, since a service charge is automatically added to most bills, it is nevertheless customary to leave a little extra. Where a service charge is not included, a tip of about ten per cent is usual for friendly and efficient service. It is not necessary to tip drivers of *dolmus* taxis, but with drivers of conventional taxis it is customary to round up the fare to the nearest 100 Lira.

Tourist Offices
(For tourist bureaux in Turkey, see individual cities and sites)
TURKISH CULTURE AND INFORMATION OFFICES
Austria: Singerstr. 2/VIII, 1010 Wien (tel: 5122128/29), telex 111281 tuinfa.
Belgium: Rue Montoyer 4, 1040 Bruxelles (tel: 5138230, 5138239).
Denmark: Vesterbrogade 11A, 1620 V Copenhagen (tel: 223100, 228374).
France: 102, Champs Elysees, 75008 Paris (tel: 145627868, 145627984, 145622610), telex 290639 turktant.
Germany: Baseler Str. 37, 6000 Frankfurt Main 1 (tel: 233081/82); Karlsplatz 3/1, 80000 München 2, (tel: 594902, 594317), telex 528190 Intu D.
Great Britain: Turkish Embassy, Culture and Information Counsellor's Office, First Floor, 170–173 Piccadilly, London W1V 9DD (tel: 01-734 8681), telex 8954905, Prestel 344208, Fax 491 0773.
Italy: Piazza della Repubblica 56, 00185 Rome (tel: 462957, 4741697), telex 612131 turktant.
Japan: 33–6, 1-chome Jingumae, Shibuya-ku Tokyo (tel: 4705131, 4706380), telex 22856 embturk-j.
Kuwait: P.O. Box 15518, 35456 Deaya (tel: 2424248, 2424298), telex 46228 turkish kt.
Netherlands: Herengracht 451, 1017 BS, Amsterdam (tel: 266810, 244006), telex 15221 tanik nl.
Saudi Arabia: Medina Road, Kilo 6, Arafat st. P.O. Box 6966, Jeddah (tel: 6654578), telex 602631 Cibneb-sj.
Spain: Plaza de Espana, Torre de Madrid Piso 13, 1–3 Madrid 288008 (tel: 2487114, 2487014), telex 47277 TTRE.
Sweden: Kungsgatan 3, 11143 Stockholm (tel: 218620), telex 11083 a telekca.
Switzerland: Talstrasse 74, 8001 Zurich (tel: 2210810/12), telex 813752 cotuch.
USA: 821 United Nations Plaza, New York, N.Y. 10017 (tel: 6872194), telex 426428; 2010 Massachusetts Avenue N.W., Washington D.C. 20036 (tel: 8338411, 4299409), telex 251544 uktm-u.

Toilets
Lavatories invariably fall well short of the standards to which most holiday-makers are accustomed. Basically, the sewage outlet system outside Turkey's bigger cities simply cannot cope with quantities of lavatory paper; as a result, small bins are provided for used paper—not a practice that is particularly appealing, especially when the bins are left unemptied for a few days, as can be the case at some of the smaller hotels and *pensions*. But you are advised to conform, as blocked lavatories are just as uninviting.

LANGUAGE

Turkish is not an easy language to learn or understand, but although many Turkish people, especially the younger generation, can speak a smattering of many European languages, knowing a few words and phrases of Turkish will help. The Turkish alphabet is very similar to the Latin alphabet except for a few letters which have special pronunciation:

The uniforms of these Sultan guards have not changed in design since the 19th century

C = *j as in Cami* (mosque), pronounced Jami

c = ch as in *Foca*, pronounced Focha

g: unpronounced but serves to extend the preceding vowel, so that *dag* (mountain) is pronounced Daa

o = oe as in Goreme, pronounced Goereme

s = sh as in Kusadasi, pronounced Kushadasi

u = like the French 'tu', as in Urgup

ı = pronounced like the 'a' in the English word 'serial'

Everyday Phrases

hello *merhaba*
goodbye *allahaismarladik* (said by the person leaving)
gule gule (said by the person seeing his or her friend off)
good morning *gunaydin*
good evening *iyi aksamlar*
goodnight *iyi geceler*
please *lutfen*
thank you *tesekkur ederim*, or *mersi*
yes *evet*
no *hayir*
there is *var*
there is not *yok*
how are you? *nasilsiniz*
I am well, thank you *iyiyim, tesekkur ederim*

Numbers

1	*bir*	40	*kirk*
2	*iki*	50	*elli*
3	*uc*	60	*altmis*
4	*dort*	70	*yetmis*
5	*bes*	80	*seksen*
6	*alti*	90	*doksan*
7	*yedi*	100	*yuz*
8	*sekiz*	101	*yuz bir*
9	*dokuz*	200	*iki yuz*
10	*on*	300	*uc yuz*
11	*on bir*	1000	*bin*
20	*yirmi*	2000	*iki bin*
30	*otuz*		

The Time and the Days

when? *nezaman?*
yesterday *dun*
today *bugun*
tomorrow *yarin*
morning *sabah*
afternoon *ogleden sonra*
evening *aksam*
night *gece*
one hour *bir saat*
what is the time? *saat kac?*
at what time? *saat kacta?*

Sunday *Pazar*
Monday *Pazartesi*
Tuesday *Sali*
Wednesday *Carsamba*
Thursday *Persembe*
Friday *Cuma*
Saturday *Cumartesi*

While Travelling

airport *hava alani*
port *liman*
town centre *sehir Merkezi*
where is it? *nerede?*
is it far? *uzak mi?*
tourism bureau *turizm burosu*
repair garage *bir tamirci*
a good hotel *iyi bir otel*
a restaurant *bir lokanta*

In the Hotel

a room *bir oda*
two people *iki kisi*
a room with a bathroom *banyolu bir oda*
what is the price? *fiyati nedir?*
hot water *sicak su*
supplementary bed *ilave bir yatak*
breakfast *Kahvalti*
butter *tereyag*
coffee *kahve*
tea *cay*
milk *sut*
sugar *seker*
the bill *hesap*

Shopping

gold *altin*
silver *gumus*
leather *deri*
copper *bakir*
how much is it? *bu ne kadar?*

In the Restaurant

bread *ekmek*
water *su*
mineral water *madensuyu*
fruit juice *meyva suyu*

Refreshing cay, *Turkish tea*

wine *sarap*
beer *bira*
ice *buz*
meat *et*
mutton *koyun eti*
lamb *kuzu eti*
beef *sigir eti*
veal *dana eti*
chicken *pilic*
fish *balik*

Hors d'oeuvre *(mezeler)*
Arnavut cigeri spicy fried liver with onions
cerkez tavugu cold chicken in walnut purée with garlic
cig kofte spicy raw meatballs
tarama fish-roe salad
yaprak dolmasi stuffed vine leaves

Soups *(corbalar)*
yogurt corbasi yoghurt soup
dugun corbasi meat soup with egg yolks
iskembe corbasi tripe soup

Grills *(izgaralar)*
bonfile fillet steak
doner kebap lamb grilled on a revolving spit
pirzola lamb chops
sis kebab grilled lamb on skewers
sis kofte grilled meatballs

Pilafs
sade pilav plain rice pilaf
ic pilav rice with pine nuts, currants and onions
bulgar pilav cracked wheat pilaf

Cold vegetables in olive oil
imam bayildi split aubergine with tomatoes and onions
babakkizartrnasi fried baby marrow served with yoghurt
patlican kizartmasi fried aubergine slices with yoghurt
zeytinyagli fasulye green beans in tomato sauce

Savoury pastries *(borekler)*
signara boregi fried filo pastry filled with cheese
su boregi layers of filo pastry filled with cheese or meat
talas puff pastry filled with meat

Salads *(salatalar)*
cacik chopped cucumber in garlic-flavoured yoghurt
coban salatasi mixed tomato, pepper, cucumber and onion salad
patlican salatasi puréed aubergine salad
piyaz haricot bean and onion salad

Desserts *(tatlilar)*
baklava flaky pastry stuffed with nuts in syrup
tel kadayif shredded wheat stuffed with nuts and syrup
sutlac cold rice pudding
komposto cold stewed fruit
dondurma ice cream

Fruits *(meyvalar)*
grapes *uzum*
peaches *seftali*
plums *erik*
apricots *kayisi*
cherries *kiraz*
figs *incir*
yellow melon *kavun*
water melon *karpuz*

INDEX

accommodation (*see also individual entries*) 110–11
Ahmet III Fountain 80
Ahtamar 94
air travel (*see also individual regions*) 113, 116
Aksaray 67
Akyarlar 22–3
Alaeddin Mosque 70
Alanya 4, 46–8
Alexander the Great 28, 33, 51–2, 56, 59
Altinkum 15
Anemorium 48
Ankara 61, 62–4
Antakya 45, 48–9
Antalya 45, 49–51
Aphrodisias 42
Aqueduct of Valens 80
Archaeological Museum (Antalya) 50
Archaeological Museum (Istanbul) 78
Asclepion 32
Aspendos 52–3
Ataturk Mausoleum 63–4
Ataturk Museum 78
Ayasofya 76–7
Ayvalik 13, 16

banks 119
beaches *see individual entries*
Bergama 32
Beyazit Tower 80
Beylerbeyi Palace 76
birdlife 97–106, 107, 108
Bitez 22
Blue Grotto 47
Blue Mosque 71, 74, 79
Bodrum 17–20
Bodrum Peninsula 20–3
Bogdogan Kemeri 80
Bosphorus 98–9, 100–1
Bursa 87–8
buses 116
Buyukada 86

Calis 31
Cappadocia 61, 64–9
car hire 12, 115
Castle of St Peter 18
Caunus 25, 26
Cavustepe 96
Celsus Library 37
Cesme 13, 23–4
Church of the Golden Headed Virgin 92
Cinili Kosk 78
Citadel (Ankara) 62
Cleopatra and Mark Antony 32, 45, 58, 59
Cleopatra's Island 41
climate 94, 112
Column of Julian 64
Cotton Castle 15
currency 118
customs regulations 115–16

Dalyan Delta 25–6
Dalyan Koy 23–4
Damlatas Cave 47
Datca 26–7
Demre 55
Derinkuyu 67–8
Didim 15–16
Dilek Peninsula 98
discounts, travel 120
Diyarbakir 94–5
Dolmabahce Palace 76
driving 11–12, 113–15, 116–17
Duden Waterfalls 53

Edirne 87
embassies 117–18
Ephesus 13, 15, 36–8
Erythrai 24–5

Fatih Mosque 79
ferries 113
festivals and events 111–12
Fethiye 28–9
Foca 13, 31–2
food and drink 109–10, 123–4
Fortress of Alanya 46
Fortress of Cesme 24

Galata Tower 80
Gallery Istanbul 85
geographical features 98, 101, 102, 103, 105
Geyre 42
Golden Horn 74
Golkoy 23
Goreme Valley 68
Grand Bazaar 12, 74, 84, 85
Green Mosque (Bursa) 87
Green Mosque (Iznik) 86
Grotto of St Peter 49
Gulf of Gokova 19
Gulf of Kusadasi 35–6
Gumbet 21

INDEX

Guvercin Adasi (Isle of Doves) 34–5
Guvercinlik 23
Guzelcamli 35–6

Haci Bayram Mosque 64
Haghia Sophia 92
Hatay Archaeological Museum 49
Herodotus 17
Heybeli 86
Hierapolis 41
Hisaronu 43
history of Turkey 6–9
Hosap 96
hotels see individual entries
House of the Virgin Mary 38
hygiene, local standards of 10, 121

Ibrahim Pasa Palace 78
Icmeler 40
Ihlara 67
Ilica 23
Istanbul 71–88, 99, 100
    monuments 79–81
    mosques 79
    museums 76–8
    palaces 75–6
Istanbul Land Walls 74, 80
Izmir 13, 32–4
Iznik 86–7

Kadifekale 33
Kadinlar 34
Kalkan 45, 53
Kaputas 53
Karaada 19
Karatay Medresesi 70
Kariye Museum 77–8
Kas 45, 53–5
Kaymakli 67–8
Kekova 55
Kemer 45, 55–6
Kilyos 90
Kizkulesi 81
Knidos 27–8
Konya 61, 69–70
Konyaalti Beach 50
Kusadasi (Island of Birds) 13, 34–6

Lake Van 93–4, 95–6
Lara Beach 50
Leander's Tower 81
local etiquette 111
loggerhead turtles 25, 107–8

Maiden's Cave 47

Mardin 95
Marmaris 38–41
Mausoleum of Halicarnassus
    (Bodrum) 19
medical insurance 118
Mersin 58
Mevlana Mausoleum 70
Miletus 38
Military Museum 78
Monastery of Sumela 89
money 118–19
Mount Ararat 93, 101
Museum of Anatolian Civilisations 63
Museum of the Ancient Orient 78
Museum of Ceramic Art (Konya) 70
Museum of Fine Arts 78
Museum of Ottoman Arms 24
Museum of Turkish Carpets 78
Museum of Turkish Ceramics
    (Istanbul) 78
Museum of Turkish and Islamic Art 78
Museum of Underwater Archaeology
    18–19
Mustafa Kemal ('Ataturk') 8–9, 62, 90
Mustafa Pasa Tower 22
Narklikuyu 48
Naval Museum 78
Nemrut Dagi 93, 94, 96
nightlife 111

Ocakkoy 43–4
Olu Deniz 42–4
Olympus 56–8
Ortakent 21–2
Ovacik 43

Pamukkale 15, 41
Paradise Island 41
Patara 30
Pergamon 7, 13, 32
Perge 51
Phaselis 56
postal services 119
Priene 38
Princes Islands 86
public baths 114
public holidays 118

rail travel (see also individual
    regions) 113, 116
Red Tower 46–7
restaurants see individual entries
road routes (see also individual
    regions) 113–14
Roman Agora (Izmir) 33

Roman Agora (Side) 59
Roman Baths (Ankara) 63
Roman Baths (Side) 59
Roman Theatre (Side) 59–60
Rumeli Hisari 80
Rustem Pasa Mosque 79

Sadberk Hanim Museum 78
St Irene Museum 78
St Paul 13, 58
St Sophia 76–7
Samsun 90–1
Sarimsakli 16
Selcuk 38
Selimye Mosque 87
shipping services (*see also individual regions*) 113, 116
shipyard (Alanya) 47
shopping (*see also individual entries*) 110
Side 45, 58–60
Sigacik 25
Sile 91
Silifke 48
Spice Bazaar 84–5
student and youth travel 119–20
Suleymaniye Mosque 79
Sultan Ahmet Square 79

Tarsus 58
Tasucu 48
taxis 116
telephones 119

Temple of Aphrodite 42
Temple of Artemis (Ephesus) 37–8
Temple of Artemis (Termessos) 52
Temple of Augustus 62–3
Temple of Zeus 52
Termessos 51–2
time, local 120
tipping 121
Tomb of the Harpies 31
Topkapi Palace 71, 74, 75–6
tourism 5, 10–11
tourist offices 121
Trabzon 89, 91–2
Troy 88
Turgutreis 21
Uludag Mountain 87, 88
Uludag National Park 106–7
underground cities (Cappadocia) 67–8
Urgup 66, 68

vaccinations 118
Van 96
Velvet Castle 33
voltage 117

wildlife 97–108
words and phrases 122–4

Xanthos 30–1

Yalova 86
Yildiz Palace 76

The Automobile Association would like to thank the following photographers and libraries for their assistance in the compilation of this book.

J ALLAN CASH PHOTOLIBRARY Cover Blue Mosque Istanbul, 11 Peasants, 13 Temple of Apollo, 22 Bitez, 25 Cesme Harbour, 45 Kalkan, 49 Hatay Museum Mosaic, 65 Mother & Child, 83 Street trader, 87 Green Mosque, 88 Troy, 94/5 Lake Van, 116/7 Nomads, 120 Mardin, 122 Sultan guards, 124 Turkish tea.

MARY EVANS PICTURE LIBRARY 12 Grand Bazaar.

INTERNATIONAL PHOTOBANK 4 Alanya, 20 Souvenirs, 59 Side, 80 Rumeli Hisari Castle, 109 Cooking & selling fish.

NATURE PHOTOGRAPHERS LTD 99 Geckos, 105 Painted frog, 107 Butterflies (R Bush), 97 Tree, 104 Turkish farm (N A Callow), 100 Red-footed falcon, 103 Woodpecker (C H Gomersall), 102 Brown Bear (W S Paton), 108 Turtle (J Sutherland), 98 Slender billed gulls (R Tidman).

SPECTRUM COLOUR LIBRARY 7 Pergamon, 17 Bodrum, 18/19 Bodrum Harbour & Castle, 26/7 Lycian cave & tombs, 29 Tombs nr. Fethiye, 30 Xanthos, 32/3 Izmir Bay, 35 Kusadasi, 36 Ephesus, 39 Marmaris, 41 Pamukkale, 50/1 Antalya, 52 Seljuk bridge, 54 Carpets in Kas, 57 Temple doorway, 61 Cappadocia, 63 Ankara, 66 Urgup, 68 Rock house Goreme, 69 Alaeddin Mosque, 79 Blue Mosque, 89 Sile, 92 Trabzon, 93 Nemrut Dagi, 113 Olu Deniz, 114 Baker's boy, 119 Shoeshine boy.

ZEFA PICTURE LIBRARY (UK) LTD 42/3 Olu Deniz, 71 Across the Bosphorus, 75 Topkapi Palace, 76/7 Sancta Sophia, 85 Grand Bazaar, 111 Grand Theatre.